CULTURES OF THE WORLD®

SAUDI ARABIA

Hunt Janin/Margaret Besheer

BENCHMARK BOOKS

MARSHALL CAVENDISH
NEW YORK

PRECEDING PAGE
Two Saudi Arabian children dressed in traditional finery.

Marshall Cavendish Corporation
99 White Plains Road
Tarrytown, NY 10591
Website: www.marshallcavendish.com

Originated and designed by
Times Books International, an imprint of
Times Media Private Limited, a member of
Times International Publishing

Printed in Malaysia

Library of Congress Cataloging-in-Publication Data
Janin, Hunt, 1940-
Saudi Arabia / by Hunt Janin and Margaret Besheer.— 2nd ed.
      p. cm.—(Cultures of the world)
   Includes bibliographical references and index.
   Contents: Geography — History — Government — Economy — Environment — Saudi Arabians — Lifestyle — Religion — Language — Arts —Leisure — Festivals — Food — Map of Saudi Arabia — About the economy — About the culture — Time line.
   ISBN 0-7614-1666-8
   1. Saudi Arabia—Juvenile literature. [1. Saudi Arabia.] I. Besheer, Margaret. II. Title. III. Series.
DS204.25.J36 2003
953.8—dc21   2003006931

7 6 5 4 3

CONTENTS

A sculpture adorns a street in Jeddah.

A Saudi and his camel, the "ship of the desert."

INTRODUCTION

AT THE CROSSROADS of the world since ancient times, the Kingdom of Saudi Arabia has grown from a land of nomadic peoples into a modern nation in the 20th century. Under the visionary leadership of a man with no formal education but with a desire to see his people prosper, Saudi Arabia has accomplished a great deal for a nation that was only truly born in 1932.

Today the Kingdom is an important industrial country, laying claim to one quarter of the world's proven oil reserves. This wealth has afforded Saudi Arabia the ability to build a very modern nation offering its citizens a variety of services.

As the birthplace of Islam, Saudi Arabia is the spiritual homeland of more than one billion people around the world.

One of Saudi Arabia's most impressive accomplishments has been its ability to preserve its rich historical past while moving forward into the 21st century.

GEOGRAPHY

SAUDI ARABIA is a vast country. Occupying four-fifths of the Arabian Peninsula it has an area of 865,000 square miles (2,240,350 square km), which is nearly a quarter the size of the United States. Saudi Arabia borders Jordan, Iraq, and Kuwait to the north, Yemen and Oman to the south, and the Persian Gulf, Qatar, and the United Arab Emirates to the east. It is separated from Egypt, Sudan, and Eritrea by the Red Sea on the west.

Seen in its geographical entirety, Saudi Arabia is a huge, tilted plateau that rises sharply from the Red Sea in the west and then slopes gradually down to the Persian Gulf in the east. It is a land of extremes. The interior of the country contains many sharp mountain ridges and great areas of sand. Saudi Arabian mountains rise to more than 9,000 feet (2,743 m) and can be freezing cold in winter. They tower above sand or gravel deserts where summer temperatures often exceed 120°F (49°C) and where it rarely rains. There are no lakes, no permanent rivers, no big forests—Saudi Arabia is probably the driest large country on the face of the earth. It is not an easy or a soft land, but it does have an austere beauty of its own.

Left: **Desert plateaus rise from a sea of sand in the northwestern region of Saudi Arabia.**

Opposite: **Curving sand dunes are caused by winds blowing through Saudi Arabia's vast deserts. The greatest area of sand in the world is found here, in the vast Rub al-Khali Desert.**

7

All the oil of the Gulf states—Iran, Iraq, Saudi Arabia, Kuwait, Bahrain, Qatar, and the United Arab Emirates—comes from the same geological formation known as the Arabian Platform. Together, these countries contain more than half of the world's proven oil reserves.

GEOLOGICAL HISTORY

Africa and the Arabian Peninsula were once fused together. About 70 million years ago, heat and stresses within the earth caused this land mass to split at the rift line now marked by the Red Sea. The Arabian part moved to the northeast. The Red Sea edge of the peninsula rose sharply, forming the western Hijaz mountains; the rest of the peninsula sloped east toward the Persian Gulf. Later, fiery lava fields covered much of the tilted Hijaz.

The low eastern areas under water received sedimentary deposits. This explains why oil is found chiefly in Al-Hasa or under the waters of the Gulf. Oil comes from the billions of tiny plants and animals that died millions of years ago, raining down upon the sea floor to form sedimentary beds.

Arab men look out onto the vast Hijaz mountains.

THE FOUR MAIN REGIONS

Saudi Arabia contains four main geographic regions: the Najd, Hijaz, Al-Hasa, and Asir.

NAJD With an average elevation of 2,000 to 3,000 feet (610 to 914 m) above sea level, the Najd is a vast eroded plateau located in the central heartland of Saudi Arabia. Much of the Najd is desert: the Nafud Desert in the north, ad-Dahna in the east, and part of the immense Rub al-Khali in the south.

The Najd is the traditional home of the ruling Saud family. Saudi Arabia's bustling capital, Riyadh, once a sleepy mud-walled village, is located here. The nomads of the Najd are known for their generosity, bravery, and love of poetry.

Eroded rocks in the Hijaz remain in place despite the ravages of time and human activity. The Hijaz has two zones, a narrow coastal plain and a mountain area. The latter has *wadis* (valleys normally dry but carrying runoff water in the rainy season) that make plant life possible.

9

HIJAZ The Hijaz has the greatest variety of people, ranging from desert Arabs to the descendants of Africans. It is the most geographically diverse region and lies in the west, in the range of mountains running parallel to the Red Sea coast. The Hijaz contains the narrow coastal strip known as the Tihamah, where the port of Jeddah is located. More importantly, the Hijaz contains the two holiest cities of Islam: Mecca and Medina.

The highlands of Asir have sustained a settled population from ancient times. Watered by the Indian Ocean monsoon, Asir is the most fertile area in Saudi Arabia.

AL-HASA Al-Hasa embraces the flat eastern coast of Saudi Arabia along the Persian Gulf. This region has lush oases, where farmers tend vividly green gardens in the midst of the desert. Most of Saudi Arabia's oil is found here, as are the great oil cities of Dhahran and Dammam. Much of Saudi Arabia's oil is shipped to world consumers by tankers loaded at Ras Tanura on the Gulf. Al-Hasa has a population of 600,000, most of them Shi'a Muslims.

ASIR Mountainous Asir is in the southwestern corner of Saudi Arabia near neighboring Yemen. Because its relatively generous rainfall made terraced agriculture possible, Asir was known to the ancient Romans as *Arabia Felix*, meaning "happy" or "flourishing" Arabia. Asir's major city is Abha, perched at an elevation of around 8,000 feet (2,428 m).

THE EMPTY QUARTER

Known as the Empty Quarter, the Rub al-Khali, in the southeastern corner of Saudi Arabia, is the greatest continuous expanse of sand in the world. About the size of the state of Texas, it covers approximately 264,000 square miles (683,760 square km)—roughly one-third of the entire country. Virtually uninhabited and subjected to blistering heat in summer days and below-freezing temperatures in winter nights, the Empty Quarter is one of the driest and most desolate places on the face of the earth.

Some of the sand in this gigantic desert stays put, but much of it is blown about into curving dunes by the incessant, ever-shifting winds. Seen from above, a typical sand dune assumes a U shape, like a huge horseshoe. Some of these sand dunes can reach a height of 330 feet (100 m).

CLIMATE

Saudi Arabia's climate differs from one part of the country to another. The country has a dry climate, with high temperatures in summer in most areas and particularly high temperatures in the central and northern areas. In the south, however, the temperature is normally moderate, dropping on the Sarawat mountains in Asir to as low as 50°F (10°C) in summer. In winter, temperatures generally become moderate, turning cold at night, when it sometimes drops to below freezing, especially on the western mountains and along the northern borders.

Because of climatic patterns, rain-bringing weather usually bypasses the Arabian Peninsula. Rainfall in most parts of Saudi Arabia is therefore uneven and unreliable. On the average, less than 4 inches (10 cm) of rain falls on Jeddah, Riyadh, or Dhahran each year. But this figure masks big regional variations.

The real pattern is usually one of drought or cloudburst. Along the Red Sea coast, torrential rains can fall in March and April. The highlands of Asir can get more than 20 inches (51 cm) of monsoon rain per year. At the other extreme, however, a desert can go without any rain at all for 10 consecutive years. Still, when rain does come to this parched land, the results are magical: seeds hidden dormant in the earth for years suddenly bloom in a matter of hours, and the apparently lifeless desert turns green for a few days.

Right: **The date palm has always played a very important role in the life of Saudi Arabians. While the wood of the tree is used for constructing houses, its fruit is used as food. As much as 600 pounds (272 kg) of fruit a year can be produced by a single date palm.**

Below: **Against the dry desert, a single flower blooms, only to wither away as quickly as it sprang to life.**

FLORA

Except for parts of rainy Asir where wild olives and some larger trees grow and the scattered oases where date palms are cultivated, there are few true trees in Saudi Arabia. The types of plants that have adapted to the harsh environment are all hardy, drought-resistant, and stunted. Most of them are brown or greenish-brown, except after infrequent rains, when patches of green herbs and colorful flowers can quickly bloom and wither. Often hundreds of consecutive square miles of the country can be covered by drought-adapted species such as the *rimth* saltbush or the yellow-flowered *arfai.* In some parts, small tamarisk and acacia trees are common.

Saudi Arabia's flora may be limited, but what is available is quite unusual. The frankincense tree, for example, produces a dried resin that used to be extremely costly. Large amounts of frankincense were burned in the religious celebrations of the ancient Middle East to perfume ceremonies and sacrifices. One shrub, known as the "toothbrush bush," is used by nomads to clean their teeth. Herbs of the desert are also used to season and preserve food, to perfume clothes, and for washing hair.

OASES

An oasis is a fertile place in a sand or gravel desert. Providing a green contrast to its dry surroundings, it is a welcome sight to weary, thirsty travelers. Some oases consist merely of a few palm trees around a spring or well. Others cover vast areas, like the Al-Hasa oasis, which is supplied by water from more than 50 artesian springs. Covering 70 square miles (182 square km), Al-Hasa includes the towns of Hofuf and Mubarraz and many villages supporting a vast permanent population. Tamarisk trees on the borders of the oasis help keep desert sand from spreading over the carefully tended gardens, which produce lush fruit, vegetables, and grains. Dates, citrus fruit, melons, tomatoes, onions, rice, wheat, barley, and henna (a plant used to make a reddish dye that women use to decorate their hands and feet and men to tint their beards) are grown here.

FAUNA

Wildlife of Saudi Arabia include the wolf, jackal, hyena, and baboon. Among the smaller animals are the fox, hedgehog, Arabian hare, jerboa (kangaroo rat), and ratel (honey badger). The gazelle, ibex, leopard, and other larger mammals were once common throughout most of Arabia, but their numbers were much diminished by overhunting in the 1930s.

Since 1986, however, Saudi Arabia's National Commission for Wildlife Conservation has set aside eight reserves to protect threatened animals and plants. The first of these to be set up was a 5,237-square mile (13,564-square km) reserve near Ta'if, not far from Jeddah. This reserve is a protected zone for endangered gazelles and the reintroduced oryx that became extinct in the wild in the early 1960s.

Birds are a common sight in the Kingdom. Large numbers of flamingoes, storks, swallows, and other birds cross the Arabian Peninsula during their annual migrations. Some winter in Saudi Arabia. Native birds include sand grouse, larks, bustards, quails, eagles, and buzzards. Gulls, pelicans, and other water birds live along the coasts.

Many species of snakes, lizards, and scorpions abound in the desert region. Domesticated animals include the camel (the chief support of nomadic life in the desert), horse, sheep, goat, and donkey.

Camels are magnificently adapted to life in the harsh desert and can go for long periods without drinking. They have heavy eyelids and long eyelashes to protect them from the sun and sand.

THE CORAL GARDEN OF THE RED SEA

Saudi Arabia's seas offer unparalleled panoramas of underwater life. The brilliantly colored marine life of the long and narrow Red Sea—about 1,150 miles (1,851 km) long and 180 miles (290 km) wide—is a spectacular example of Saudi Arabia's natural beauty.

The clear, warm, shallow areas of this body of water provide the perfect environment for the growth of corals, which come in a wide range of sizes, shapes, and colors. Their names suggest their rich diversity: there are hard, soft, black, fire (these can sting divers badly), brain (shaped like a giant human brain), mushroom, bushy, and fan corals. Seen under water, these formations are so abundant and so beautiful that they are often referred to as "coral gardens."

To swim over the crest of a Red Sea reef while wearing a face mask and to look down at the bottom through 30 feet (55 m) of clear, warm, sunlit water is to see an unforgettable, colorful profusion of marine life. Among the harmless and most brightly colored fish in the coral gardens are parrotfish, butterfly fish, pennant fish, royal angelfish, and coral trout. Some less common and more dangerous creatures include lionfish, stonefish, stingrays, moray eels, and sharks.

CITIES OF THE KINGDOM

The major urban areas of Saudi Arabia are Riyadh, the capital, located in the interior; Jeddah, a key port and commercial center on the Red Sea; the Dhahran/Dammam/Al Khobar complex, the center of oil production, near the Gulf coast; and Mecca and Medina, the two holiest cities of Islam, located in the western hills of the Hijaz.

RIYADH When Abdul Aziz, founder of the Kingdom of Saudi Arabia, captured Riyadh in a camel raid in 1902, it was a tiny mud-brick village in the wilderness of central Arabia. It remained something of a backwater until the sharp run-up of oil prices after 1973 turned it into a boom town. The Saudis then wanted to modernize their capital. They succeeded so well that Riyadh has grown more quickly than any other city in the Middle East. In less than 50 years, Riyadh was transformed from a mud-walled town of 25,000 inhabitants into an international metropolis of more than three million people.

An aerial view of Riyadh, the political and economic center of the nation.

Today Riyadh is a sprawling urban city highlighted by a combination of modernist and traditional Arab architecture. Many modern convieniences are readily available, as is air conditioning. Reflecting Riyadh's importance as a world capital, the entire diplomatic corps moved there from Jeddah in the 1980s. There are now about 90 embassies and other diplomatic missions in Riyadh, all located in a separate diplomatic enclave near the city. The city is served by the King Khalid International Airport, which was opened in 1983. Since 2002 the capacity of the airport has doubled to accommodate 15 million passengers.

JEDDAH Traditionally known as the "Bride of the Red Sea," Jeddah is an ancient commercial port that handled much of the spice trade of the Red Sea and served as the gateway for pilgrims coming to nearby Mecca. Like Riyadh, Jeddah also grew explosively during the oil boom. The old harbor, which had become a bottleneck for the entry of badly needed building materials and consumer items, was rebuilt into a modern port capable of handling 22.6 million tons (2 billion kg) of freight each year. A new airport covering 40 square miles (104 square km)—the King Abdul Aziz International Airport—was constructed to ease the entry into the Kingdom of more than 1.5 million Muslim pilgrims each year. The population of Jeddah is now about 2.5 million people. Many residents think their city is more charming than Riyadh, even if it lacks the capital's political and financial importance.

DHAHRAN/DAMMAM/AL KHOBAR This port-city complex consisting of Dhahran, Dammam, and Al Khobar has also experienced rapid growth in recent years. It is the home of the Arabian-American Oil Company (now owned by the Saudis and known as Saudi Aramco) and of the University of Petroleum and Minerals. The three oil cities, with a population of about 500,000, serve as an outlet to the world for the vast petroleum-gathering and petrochemical industries of the Al-Hasa region. King Fahd International Airport serves this booming region.

MECCA Formerly a market town for camel caravans, Mecca is the birthplace of Islam. Throughout its history, Mecca has been venerated as a holy place and has attracted Arabs from every part of the Arabian Peninsula, as well as Muslims from around the world. When the annual tide of *hajj* (HAHJ) pilgrims floods in, Mecca's population temporarily approaches two million. Normally, however, the city is much smaller, with a population of about 850,000. Mecca contains the Grand Mosque, where the great Ka'bah (kah-AH-bah), the holiest shrine of Islam and the focal point of Islamic worship, is located.

Medina Railway Station is a striking example of traditional Arabic architecture.

MEDINA After Mecca, Medina is the second most important city for Muslims. It is where Prophet Muhammad, Islam's founder, took refuge from the persecution occuring in Mecca. Medina's most venerated historic site is Muhammad's tomb, located in the Prophet's mosque. Medina also houses an Islamic University and the famous King Abdul Aziz Library, which contains a huge collection of some 37,000 books on religious topics, as well as a collection of rare copies of the Koran, some in the form of manuscripts written hundreds of years ago. Medina has a population of about 430,000.

HISTORY

CIVILIZATION IN THE ARABIAN PENINSULA goes back many thousands of years. If there is any pattern evident over this long stretch of time, it is that periods when each region or nomadic group was a law unto itself have alternated with periods of dynastic control. The unsettled conditions during the decline of the ruling Ottoman empire, for example, were brought to an end by the founding of the modern kingdom of Saudi Arabia in 1932.

Ancient Saudi history is relatively difficult to find from an archeological perspective, partly because the desert sand has buried much of the country's ancient treasures. Ruins that are found are usually remarkably preserved because of the dry, arid climate.

Opposite: **A building in a deserted town in ancient Dedan in northwestern Saudi Arabia. Situated along a major caravan route, Dedan was an important city serving the spice trade.**

THE COMING OF THE PROPHET

The most important event, and turning point, in the history of the Arabian Peninsula was the birth of Prophet Muhammad, the founder of Islam, in A.D. 571. When the Prophet was born, his home town of Mecca was already a sacred place of worship of pagan gods.

Within his lifespan Prophet Muhammad established a religion that was destined for a world role and laid the foundations of the Arab empire. Preaching the oneness of Allah, he became the temporal and spiritual leader, as the Islamic faith substituted traditional tribal loyalties for the religious bond. A century later, the Arabs, carrying the message of Islam, rode out of Arabia and conquered a large part of the civilized world.

THE EARLIEST ARABS

In prehistoric times, Stone Age hunter-gatherers drifted out of eastern Africa into the Arabian Peninsula, which was then lush and well-watered. About 15,000 years ago, however, the weather grew warmer and the deserts began to spread. Some of the inhabitants became nomads herding camels, goats, and sheep. Others settled in small villages around oases or along the sea coasts and supported themselves by agriculture and trade.

Wedged between three major continents, the Arabian Peninsula was an important passage for caravans of traders crisscrossing the vast deserts, carrying frankincense and myrrh, silk and spices, gold, precious stones, and ivory to Egypt, Palestine, Syria, and ancient Babylon. Many of the early inhabitants of Arabia performed the important role of middlemen in this commercial link.

One group, called the Nabateans, settled in the northwestern part of Arabia, where they built a stronghold at Madain Salih to control this trade. In A.D. 106, however, the Romans captured the capital at Petra to strengthen their own hold on the trade routes of Arabia. This military conquest marked the begining of the decline of the Nabatean civilization.

Arabia continued to be a commercial crossroads, but infighting among the Arab groups for control of the trade routes resulted in instability within the area that eventually led to a general decline in trade and business. By A.D. 200, parts of northern Saudi Arabia had been incorporated into the Roman province of Arabia. In the fourth and sixth centuries, southwestern Arabia fell

An old fort stands on a caravan route.

20

under Abyssinian rule. Throughout all these years Arabia remained politically fragmented. By the beginning of the sixth century, it was still a collection of small warring states.

MUHAMMAD AND ISLAM

Mecca, where Muhammad was born, was a trading center for the camel caravans bringing goods along the Red Sea coast. Muhammad's parents died when he was young. Until age eight, he was raised by his grandfather. At the death of his grandfather, Muhammad's guardian was his uncle Abu Talib.

Muhammad himself was poor, but his prospects rose when, at about age 25, he married a rich widow 15 years his senior. Although he was a good trader, Muhammad also had a strong religious inclination. When he reached his 40s, he would retreat to a cave outside Mecca to pray and meditate on ways to improve the morality of his society. Tradition says it was there that the archangel Gabriel revealed to him the word of God.

Muhammad's first convert was his wife Khadija. By about A.D 613 he was publicly preaching about what had been revealed to him. His followers wrote down what he said and in so doing gradually compiled a holy book, the Koran, which they believed had been dictated to Muhammad by God. Other Meccans, however, strenuously objected to his teachings because it threatened to stop the *jinn* worship at the Ka'bah and thus hurt Mecca financially. To escape persecution, in A.D 622, Muhammad and some of his followers moved to a neighboring city, first known as Yathrib and later as Medina. This emigration now marks the starting point of the Muslim calendar.

Muhammad's great talents propelled him into a commanding military and political position in Medina. In A.D 630, his forces conquered Mecca, where he transformed the Ka'bah into a shrine for Muslims and treated the vanquished Meccans with dignity and honor. Most of them soon became followers of Islam. When Muhammad died in A.D 632, he had founded what was shortly to become a new world religion.

The ruins of an old mosque on an ancient trade route show its simple mud and brick architecture.

THE EXPANSION OF ISLAM

By the time Muhammad died in A.D. 632, the unification of the Arabian Peninsula was underway. Later, under the Umayyad dynasty (A.D 661–750), which ruled from Damascus, Islam spread rapidly, eventually reaching west into Spain and North Africa, north into Syria and Mesopotamia, and east into Afghanistan and parts of India.

But financial problems and feuding among Arab tribes weakened this dynasty, and it was soon overthrown. In its place arose the Abbasid dynasty (A.D 750–1258) who ruled from Baghdad and made it the capital city. Baghdad soon became a world center of wealth and military power between the ninth and eleventh centuries, reaching a peak of glory under the rule of the fifth caliph, Harun al-Rashid and his son. But a gradual economic decline set in, sealing the fate of the Abbasids. In 1258 the Mongols sacked Baghdad: the last caliph was kicked to death, and the streets of the city were piled high with corpses.

FOREIGN RULE

The Mamluks were a military caste that ruled Egypt from 1250 to 1517. During the 14th and 15th centuries they also controlled the Hijaz, including Mecca, Medina, and Jeddah. In 1517, however, the Ottoman sultan, Selim I, conquered Egypt and assumed control of the Hijaz. His successor, Suleiman the Magnificent, spent huge amounts of money on fabulous new buildings for the holy cities of Islam.

In time, the Ottoman empire weakened. Two important figures arose in the Najd, the heartland of the nomads. The first was an 18th-century Muslim preacher, Muhammad bin Abdul Wahhab. He wanted to purify Islam and rid it of the local customs and mystical influences that in his view had tainted it badly.

The second was a local sheikh of the Najd, Muhammad bin Saud, who wanted to protect and expand the territory his people controlled. The ambitions of these two men dovetailed nicely, and in about 1750 they decided to join forces.

SETBACKS AND TRIUMPH

The sons of Muhammad bin Saud and Muhammad bin Abdul Wahhab continued the ambitious plan of expansion their fathers had begun. By 1804 they had taken control of the holy cities of Mecca and Medina and had established a political-religious state embracing almost one million square miles (2.6 million square km) of the Arabian Peninsula.

Their very success prompted the Ottoman Empire to send forces to retake the region. The Ottoman army recaptured the holy cities and, in about 1818, had also captured the ancestral home of the Saud family in the Najd. Thus the House of Saud's first effort to found a kingdom ended in a dismal failure.

A second effort began in about 1820 but it, too, failed—this time because a rival family, the Rashid dynasty, eventually seized Riyadh from Saud control in 1891 and forced the Saud family to flee to neighboring Kuwait. There the family waited for the opportunity to regain its lost lands. This chance finally came in 1902 when Abdul Aziz Ibn Saud (also known as Ibn Saud, son of Saud) led 40 companions into the desert and, in a daring camel-back raid, captured Riyadh after fierce hand-to-hand fighting.

The foundations of modern Saudi Arabia were laid by King Abdul Aziz Ibn Saud. Under his rule, Arabia was transformed from a country of divided tribal allegiances into a unified nation.

Abdul Aziz Ibn Saud was a very tall, physically powerful, and highly intelligent leader. He was a devout Muslim and spent part of each day in prayer and religious reading. To win the allegiance of the scattered, independent desert groups, he briefly married and then divorced (strictly in keeping with the customs of Islam—by not having more than four wives at a time) a very large number of women.

Abdul Aziz himself claimed that he had married more than 282 women and had fathered over 46 sons and many daughters. By the time of his death it was clear he had fathered at least 58 officially recorded sons and an unrecorded number of daughters. These offspring form the core of the huge royal family of today.

THE UNIFICATION OF SAUDI ARABIA

The headquarters of T.E. Lawrence at Azraq Castle in Jordan during World War I.

After capturing Riyadh, Abdul Aziz spent the next decade fighting the Rashid dynasty, who had the support of the Ottomans. He did not meet with much success. He finally hit on the idea of uniting the nomads and encouraging them to settle down. This he did by creating a religious brotherhood, which he called the *Ikhwan* (ik-WAHN), or brethren. The *Ikhwan* spread the puritanical Wahhabi gospel favored by most of the nomads.

In 1914, backed by *Ikhwan* fighters, Abdul Aziz captured most of central Arabia and the Eastern Province and pushed the Ottomans from the Gulf coastline. At this time, however, the western region, the Hijaz, was under the rule of another rival, Hussein. Enlisting the help of the British adventurer and soldier T.E. Lawrence, Hussein defeated the Ottomans at Aqaba and proclaimed himself king of the Hijaz. The conflict between Hussein and Abdul Aziz for supremacy was inevitable. In 1925, after years of fighting, Abdul Aziz conquered the Hijaz region. In 1932 he unified Al-Hasa, the Najd, and the Hijaz into a new country known as the Kingdom of Saudi Arabia.

LAWRENCE OF ARABIA

During World War I, the Arabs launched a revolt in Mecca to expel the Ottomans and their German allies from the Middle East. But the Ottomans rallied quickly and sent men and supplies from Syria down the Hijaz railroad to Medina. The British had promised to help the Arabs attack the Turks. A young British archeologist-turned-intelligence officer, Captain Thomas Edward Lawrence, rallied the different Arab tribes together and led them to battle.

In his famous and beautifully written account of this campaign, entitled *Seven Pillars of Wisdom*, Lawrence described his experiences leading up to the eventual victory of the Bedouin forces over the Ottomans. In 1917, together with about 30 camel-mounted nomads, he set out through the searing heat of the Hijaz mountains in northwestern Saudi Arabia to capture the strategic port of Aqaba, at the northern tip of the Red Sea. In a surprise attack by land, after a grueling trip through the desert, Lawrence and the Arabs succeeded in capturing Aqaba. This battle, though small, was key in preventing the Ottomans from assuming control over Arabia.

THE DEVELOPMENT OF A MODERN STATE

Saudi Arabia's stability owes much to the fact that a single dynasty has governed since Abdul Aziz Ibn Saud established the Kingdom in 1932. This was further enhanced by the discovery of oil in 1938, as oil wealth made it possible for King Abdul Aziz to begin the country's transformation into a modern state.

Saud, the eldest son of Abdul Aziz, became king when his father died in 1953. In 1964 King Saud abdicated in favor of his brother, Faisal, who ruled until his assassination in 1975. Faisal's rule saw the implementation of a program that started Saudi Arabia's drive toward modernization. Faisal was succeeded as king by his half-brother, Khalid. Economic development continued rapidly, thanks to the rapid rise of oil prices. More significantly, King Khalid's reign set in motion the Second Development Plan, which brought further improvements in the people's economic and social standards of living.

When King Khalid died in 1982, his brother Fahd became the fourth and present king. King Fahd continues to lead the economic developement of the country through initiations to diversify the economy.

During the short, sharp conflict in the Gulf, in which the ground fighting itself lasted only 100 hours, more than 600,000 troops from 37 countries were deployed to Saudi Arabia.

FOREIGN POLICY

Saudi Arabia has traditionally been on very good terms with Western countries, especially the United States. During the Cold War, Saudi Arabia had no formal relations with the Soviet Union, as it opposed the beliefs of communism.

Saudi Arabia has become an important mediator of regional conflicts. One of its most important foreign policy goals is to see a peaceful resolution to the conflict between the Palestinians and the Israelis. In March 2002, at a meeting of the Arab League, Crown Prince Abdullah put forth a plan for separate Israeli and Palestinian states to peacefully coexist. Saudi Arabia continues to play an active role in seeking a realistic resolution of the enmity between the two peoples.

THE GULF WAR

Iraq's unprovoked attack on its neighbor, Kuwait, in August 1990, posed a dilemma for Saudi Arabia. Both the Saudis and the Americans feared that Iraq would try to capture the oil fields in the eastern part of the Kingdom.

The Saudis recognized that they did not have the military power needed to stop an invasion by Iraq. King Fahd decided that the wisest course of action was to join forces with the Americans and their allies in hopes of defeating Iraq as quickly as possible.

Thus, five days after the Iraqi attack on Kuwait, U.S. troops began to arrive in Saudi Arabia. In November 1990, the United Nations Security Council authorized the use of "all necessary means" to expel Iraq from Kuwait. When Iraq failed to withdraw, the Gulf War began in January 1991. The war cost the Saudi government an estimated $37.5 billion. Without Saudi Arabia's full military and financial cooperation, the United States and its allies could not have won the war so quickly.

TERRORISM IN THE 21ST CENTURY

Terrorism has become a fact of life in the 21st century. Every country has been affected by it or the threat of it. People from more than 60 nations were killed in the attacks on the World Trade Center in New York on September 11, 2001.

Saudi Arabia feels the sting of terrorism particularly strongly. Fifteen of the 19 hijackers aboard the airliners that crashed in New York, Virginia, and Pennsylvania in 2001 were Saudi citizens. Because of this, the Kingdom has been criticized for not having done enough to stop religious fervor from growing within its borders.

Osama bin Laden, the leader of the al-Qaeda terrorist network and the man believed to be behind the September 11 attacks, is originally a Saudi citizen. However, because of his fanatic beliefs that run counter to the teachings of Islam, Saudi Arabia stripped him of his citizenship in 1994.

Saudi Arabia has also been the victim of terrorism on its shores. In 1996 an apartment building complex in eastern Saudi Arabia housing U.S. military personnel was attacked by a truck carrying explosives. Nineteen Americans were killed at the Khobar Towers (*above*). Saudi Arabia worked hard in cooperation with the United States to bring the perpetrators to justice.

The Kingdom strongly condemns acts of terrorism, saying that they are forbidden by Islam. The government actively pursues an anti-terrorism policy and works with the United States and the international community in the war on terrorism. Nevertheless, rumors maintain that terrorist training camps operate within its borders.

GOVERNMENT

SAUDI ARABIA IS A MONARCHY with the Koran as its constitution. The king heads the government as the prime minister and also as president of the Council of Ministers.

The present king of Saudi Arabia is, by title and full name, the "Custodian of the Two Holy Mosques, King Fahd bin Abdul Aziz Al Saud." He is the fifth king of the royal House of Saud.

The king combines in his person all the major functions of government—executive, legislative, and judicial. In the tradition of the desert, however, sheikhs could never wield absolute power. They were chosen by their people as the best men for the job, and they had to rule in accordance with public opinion. An informal but well-understood set of checks and balances helps to keep the Saudi kings in their proper role, which is to lead the country and to stay in contact with their people.

Saudi Arabia is not governed by a written constitution but by a body of Islamic law called *sharia* (SHAH-ree-ah). This body of law, refined through the centuries by Muslim legal scholars, is based on the Koran and the example of the Prophet. Strict adherence to *sharia* law is ensured by the Muslim *ulema* (oo-ley-MAH), Wahhabi clerics, who advise the king on the application of *sharia* law from issues such as law-making to handing out punishment for offences. The inclusion of the Wahhabi clerics in governance is a holdover from the alliance between the Wahhabis and the House of Saud that eventually led to the unification of the peninsula. The *ulema* now ensure that the king's decisions, while having the final authority, must adhere to the *sharia* law, which makes clear the duty of a political and religious leader: he must rule for the common good. To keep the king's power and activity in check, his decisions must have the consensus of not only the *ulema*, but the royal family and important members of the Saudi public as well.

Above: **Widely known for his interest in education, King Fahd has adopted an enlightened approach to transform Saudi Arabia into a modern state. Under his rule, he has established Saudi Arabia as a steadying influence in world affairs.**

Opposite: **A Consultative Council meeting in Riyadh is chaired by Crown Prince Abdullah.**

Located in the diplomatic quarters of Riyadh, the Ministry of Foreign Affairs building is also situated close to the offices of the king and the Council of Ministers' Complex. All the major policy-making decisions are made here in Riyadh.

NATIONAL AND LOCAL GOVERNMENT

The king appoints a Council of Ministers, which has numerous legislative, executive, and administrative duties and a considerable say in what goes on at the national and local level. The king, however, can veto the Council's decisions and can replace its ministers at will.

The Consultative Council, inaugurated on December 29, 1993, and consisting of appointed members, shares authority with the government and advises the Council of Ministers. The members are expected to be chosen from the academic, business, and religious elite. Besides reviewing laws and government policies, the Consultative Council is empowered to recommend that the king reject those laws or policies found lacking. But the king remains the final arbiter of state affairs.

Setting up the Consultative Council meant broadening the participation of Saudi citizens in their own governments. No longer would the Saudi royal princes have a monopoly on decision-making. The number of members in the Consultative Council has increased from its initial 60 to 90, and since 2001 there are a total of 120 members.

For administrative purposes, Saudi Arabia is divided into 13 provinces. Each province has a governor, who is often a senior-ranking prince of the al-Saud family, as well as a deputy governor. The provincial governors are appointed by the King.

Each province has a council consisting of officials and private citizens. They are appointed, not elected. It is the job of the provincial councils to study local issues and present reports to the Minister of the Interior in Riyadh, who then acts on the reports as he sees fit.

Despite this apparent decentralization, however, in practice Saudi Arabia is run very much from the top down—all the important decisions are made in Riyadh. There are no self-sufficient elected local governments, as there are in the United States, at the city and state level.

In the Kingdom of Saudi Arabia, all the local administrative units depend entirely on the capital for policy guidance and for financial support. Riyadh, in turn, assumes full responsibility for supporting the provincial councils.

Apart from the election of some low-level advisors to help the chief municipal executives, there are no elections in Saudi Arabia. Furthermore, since Saudi Arabia is a monarchy, there are no political parties.

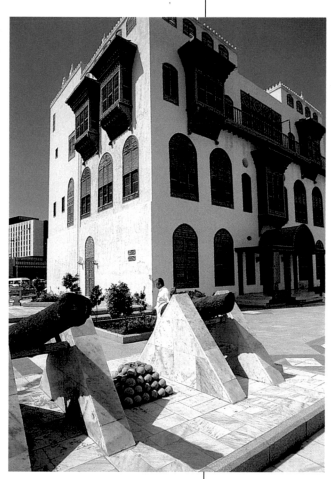

The British Legation in Riyadh. The moving of the entire diplomatic corps from Jeddah to Riyadh in the mid-1980s was an indication of the growing importance of Riyadh as a world city.

Supplicants await their turn at a *majlis* officiated by a Saudi prince.

HOW DECISIONS ARE MADE

Decisions at all levels in Saudi Arabia—national, local, tribal, or family— are made only after an informal, usually lengthy discussion and consultation. One goal is to make sure that all views are heard, not only so that good ideas will surface, but also to give everybody a chance to participate personally and have a say in the decision-making process.

Personal participation is most noticeable in the daily *majlis* (MAHJ-lis), or public audience held by high officials. Each day, for example, Prince Salman, the governor of Riyadh, reads petitions presented to him in person by a long line of supplicants. He then passes the petitions on to an aide for appropriate action.

One of the king's most important responsibilities is to find enough common ground among the different elements in the society so that a consensus can eventually be reached. Maintaining this kind of public forum in an increasingly complex society is quite challenging. Sometimes a consensus cannot be found, and the final decision must be decided and imposed from above.

KEEPING THE PEACE

Given the frequent wars in the Middle East, Saudi Arabia is lucky. It has been blessed with relative peace and stability ever since it was formally created in 1932. It has never been invaded by another country, although Iraq had apparently planned to do so at the beginning of the Gulf War in 1991. There has been one attempted insurrection, in 1979, when a religious fanatic and his followers seized the Grand Mosque in Mecca and held out for a week before being captured and executed.

Saudi Arabia's special relationship with the United States, coupled with its own armed forces, has helped to keep the peace. In addition, the Saudis have spent billions of their oil dollars on defense, investing in a highly sophisticated air defense network and buying a great deal of other advanced weaponry from the West.

A well-trained force, the Saudi National Guard plays a vital role in maintaining internal stability.

The Kingdom's armed forces are also required to defend the House of Saud itself, especially in cases of internal uprisings. This is the role of the National Guard. Historical if not literal descendants of the *Ikhwan*, who fought hard for King Abdul Aziz but were later suppressed by him, the enlisted men of the National Guard are still responsible primarily for protecting the royal family against any internal opponents. The National Guard also assists pilgrims during the *hajj* and are involved in the implementation of social programs in the country. In times of war, the National Guard will join the armed forces in combat.

ECONOMY

ORIGINALLY BASED ON subsistence agriculture and funds brought in by those entering the country for pilgrimages, the economic structure of Saudi Arabia was completely transformed by the rapid rise of oil prices in the 1970s. The Kingdom's revenue from the sale of its oil has allowed Saudi Arabia to design and finance ambitious development projects that have set world records for size and cost.

The full extent of Saudi Arabia's petroleum resources is still not known: oil companies keep finding more oil and gas. But it is clear that Saudi Arabia has roughly 25 percent of the world's proven reserves of crude oil and its gas reserves are the fourth largest in the world.

More than 95 percent of all Saudi oil is produced on behalf of the Saudi government by the Saudi Arabian Oil Company (Saudi Aramco). The Japanese-owned Arabian Oil Company and the U.S.-based Getty Oil Company (now owned by Texaco) provide the rest of Saudi crude oil production.

Affiliates of the Saudi government's General Petroleum and Minerals Organization (Petromin) handle oil refining, as well as the production and marketing of refined petroleum products. Since Saudi Arabia has few other resources and is the world's leading oil exporter, petroleum is still the mainspring of the economy, contributing two-thirds of government revenues and 90 percent of the country's export earnings.

Above and opposite: **Located to the north of Dhahran on the Gulf, Ras Tanura is the world's largest petroleum port.**

A TYPICAL WORKDAY

A typical workday for a modern middle-class Saudi family is in some respects like that of a North American family in the 1950s: the father leaves the house and goes off to work at an office; the mother usually stays home to run the household; and the children go to school.

The pace of office work is usually more relaxed in Saudi Arabia than in the United States. Less attention is paid to being physically present in the office during office hours. Saudi government offices are, in theory, open from 7:30 A.M. until 2:30 P.M., but not all officials will be there for the full period of time. Private businesses operate from 8:00 A.M. until noon and then again from 3:00 to 6:00 P.M. Markets and shops stay open until

THE DATE

In Ash Sharqiyah (Eastern Province) lies Al-Hasa, the world's largest oasis. Millions of tall, lush palm trees have stood here for thousands of years. Hanging from the lower palm fronds are giant clusters of dates. More than 300 varieties of this fruit grow in Saudi Arabia.

Dates have been a vital part of the nomad's diet throughout history. Today they are consumed by pregnant women, who need the extra nutrition, by Muslims as they break their daily fast during the holy month of Ramadan, and by anyone looking for a tasty and nutritious snack.

Before oil was discovered in the 1930s, dates were Saudi Arabia's main export. Today, the Kingdom is the world's second-largest producer, supplying nearly 20 percent of the world market, in addition to sending dates as food aid to poorer parts of the world.

The date palm is a revered symbol in Saudi culture. Its importance is evident in the national emblem: a date palm suspended over two crossed swords. The date palm represents vitality and growth, while the swords represent justice and strength.

9:00 P.M. The owners or their relatives are likely to be at their shops during most of this time.

All trading ceases during prayer times, which occur five times a day between sunrise and sunset. The first prayer is offered after dawn but before sunrise. The next prayer is roughly at noon. An afternoon prayer and two final prayers (at sunset and in the late evening) complete the religious day. During these daily prayer times, businesses all over the Kingdom close for about 20 minutes to an hour.

The Saudi weekend falls on Thursday and Friday, since Friday is the Muslim holy day.

FOREIGN WORKERS

Some five million foreigners work in Saudi Arabia. They come from countries such as Yemen, the Philippines, Sri Lanka, Egypt, Pakistan, and India. Many also come from Western Europe and the United States.

Traditionally these workers were necessary because Saudis did not have the education or technical expertise to work in certain industries, such as petrochemicals or aviation. However, reliance on foreign manpower is declining; thousands of Saudis graduate from the Kingdom's numerous universities and technical or vocational schools each year. Others are returning graduates and professionals from foreign institutions. Programs offered by local institutions form the backbone of the "Saudization" of the labor force, a campaign promoted by the Saudi government to decrease reliance on foreign manpower and to explore other sources of national income.

Foreign workers account for a large percentage of Saudi Arabia's labor force. Some work in technical and professional fields; others in construction and domestic work.

43

ENVIRONMENT

SAUDI ARABIA'S combination of vast deserts, rugged mountains, and green oases presents environmentalists with many challenges. Couple this with the harsh climate that dominates the Arabian Peninsula for most of the year, and the experts have a series of important environmental issues with which to contend.

The Kingdom has established several organizations for the purpose of protecting and preserving the country's ecosystem, such as the National Commission for Wildlife Conservation and Development. Furthermore, various academia and government bodies work together to further Saudi Arabia's tradition of environmental preservation and protection.

Below: **Palm trees grow in the arid Arabian climate. Most of the country consists of deserts.**

Opposite: **The oryx is native to the Arabian Peninsula. It has inspired many traditional poems and stories.**

ISSUES

Saudi Arabia is a highly industrialized country, where limiting and containing pollution is a high priority. In the 1970s the government established strict regulations to limit harmful emissions. These regulations affect the planning, design, construction, and operation of new factories and other industrial facilities. The success of these environmental laws in reducing air and water pollution is evident in the industrialized cities of the Kingdom.

In 1981 Saudi Arabia established the Meteorology and Environmental Protection Administration (MEPA) to improve the efficiency of national conservation efforts. One of MEPA's main tasks is to collect scientific data on the Kingdom's plant and animal species. This information provides a valuable basis for long-term environmental planning decisions, which are used especially by the industrial and defense sectors of the economy.

MEPA also monitors marine, land, and air pollution. Scientists regularly collect air, water, and soil samples from across the Kingdom to check for changes in the levels of organic and man-made pollutants. Monitoring such changes is very important for the long-term health of the people, plants, and animals of Saudi Arabia.

OIL SPILLS

Since Saudi Arabia is the world's largest producer of petroleum and petroleum products, taking special precaution to prevent oil spills is especially important. Tanker ships carrying crude and refined oil have double hulls to help prevent leaks and spills. However, accidents do occasionally occur, causing oil spills that can severely damage marine life.

During the Gulf War in 1991, the Iraqi regime deliberately caused a massive oil spill in the Persian Gulf by releasing 11 million gallons of crude oil into its waters as they retreated from Kuwait, Saudi Arabia's northern neighbor. More than 800 miles of the Saudi and Kuwaiti coastline were affected by the oil. Contingency plans prepared by Saudi authorities helped to contain the environmental damage to the coastline, and as a result minimized the loss of marine life.

Saudi Arabia is dedicated to finding new sources of renewable energy. Besides being a producer of petroleum and gas products, the Kingdom is working towards becoming a serious producer of solar energy

Left: **Oil transportation poses a significant threat to the environment. Each year, thousands of gallons of oil are accidently spilled into the Persian Gulf. This is why the government sees this as a problem and are implementing measures to control such oil spillage.**

Opposite: **Industrial areas are subject to governmental controls to reduce air and water pollution.**

The huge sandy expanse of the Rub al-Khali desert covers about half of Saudi Arabia.

DESERTIFICATION

Much of Saudi Arabia is covered in sand; in fact, the world's largest sand desert—Rub al-Khali (The Empty Quarter)—stretches across the southern part of the country. The total annual rainfall in Riyadh averages 4 inches (10 cm), and there are no permanent rivers anywhere in the country.

This combination of dry weather and sand poses a real environmental threat to Saudi Arabia's cities. The problem is known as desertification. At Riyadh's King Saud University, students and scientists at the Center for Desert Studies work to devise viable ways to keep drifting sands from encroaching into the cities. Some options for containing deserts include planting special plants, building fences, and using other means to stabilize or anchor the sand. The university dedicates much of its research to learning about the uniqueness of the desert environment. It uses that knowledge to develop programs to protect both the desert and the ecosystem that relies on it for survival. Such efforts aim to ensure the comfort of people's lives in the nearby cities.

THE KING ABDUL AZIZ CITY FOR SCIENCE AND TECHNOLOGY

One institution that has been important in the development of higher education in Saudi Arabia is the King Abdul Aziz City for Science and Technology (KACST). This organization is responsible for the administration and supervision of all scientific research projects in Saudi Arabia.

Each year, KACST awards millions of dollars in grants to scientists working on a variety of projects in the Kingdom. In addition, KACST conducts its own research projects and works on joint projects with international scientific centers. Student researchers at KACST use state of the art equipment to monitor and record scientific findings (*below*). Some of their research projects are in the fields of energy, agriculture, astronomy and aeronautics, the environment, and computers. For example, in the 1980s KACST collaborated with the United States National Aeronautics and Space Administration (NASA) to track sand drifting and underground water and to map out this information. Other such joint research projects are with Australia for astronomy and laser technology, Germany for solar energy, and Taiwan for the study of freshwater fish culture.

Since its establishment in 1978, KACST has been the driving force behind Saudi Arabia's technological development. Strong government support reflects the importance the government places on the development of science and technology.

CONSERVATION

Saudi Arabia's heritage is deeply embedded in the idea of living in harmony with nature. Out of this nomadic heritage, the Saudis have developed a great respect and affection for the fragility of nature. They are raised to believe that it is their social responsibility to care for and protect all endangered species from organic and man-made threats. Furthermore, Islam teaches that all living things are created with value and purpose and that it is the responsibility of human beings to conserve and protect the natural environment.

In 1986, by royal decree, the government established the National Commission for Wildlife Conservation and Development (NCWCD) for this purpose. More than 100 areas have been designated for endangered plants and animals, protecting them from hunters and poachers. These areas extend to the Red Sea and the Persian Gulf.

The NCWCD has also reintroduced animals that have become extinct in certain regions back into their original habitats. At the Mahazat Al-Sayd

Reserve in southwestern Saudi Arabia, one of the 15 reserves established and cared for by the NCWCD, breeders have successfully reintroduced the wild Arabian oryx, which vanished from the area more than a decade ago. Scientists were able to bring the wild Arabian oryx from other parts of the Kingdom and start herds in the new habitat. The oryx population has since increased by about 13 percent. Another important conservation effort is the restoration of mangroves that have been damaged or are deteriorating.

SOLAR ENERGY

Although Saudi Arabia is the world's largest exporter of oil and a major producer of natural gas, the Kingdom is working to explore alternative energy sources. With 105 trillion kilowatt-hours of sunshine—the energy equivalent of 10 billion barrels of oil—beating down on its surface each day, Saudi Arabia has naturally turned its research efforts toward solar power.

Solar power is a good alternative energy for remote areas, such as the desert or mountains. King Abdul Aziz University in Jeddah, in conjunction with the United States Department of Energy, has developed one of the world's largest solar-powered electricity-generating systems. The generator provides electricity to several remote villages in Saudi Arabia. A solar dish absorbs the sun's energy and converts it to electricity (*right*).

Other solar research includes trying to find ways to harness the sun's energy to benefit agriculture, to desalinate water, and to power communications equipment. Alternative sources of energy are becoming increasingly important as Saudi Arabai's oil fields are steadily being depleted.

SAUDI ARABIANS

MANY SAUDI ARABIANS are direct descendants of the ancient nomads, whose name has come down through the ages as *Aribi* or *Arabu* and who are now known as Arabs. The early Arabs lived in the northern deserts of the Arabian Peninsula. Some of them settled near oases and others remained nomadic.

The isolation of desert life kept the ancestral Arabs from mingling and mixing with other peoples, with the result that many Saudis are considered to be "pure" Arabs. One sign of this is that they are very similar physically and presumably, resemble their nomad ancestors. The rigors of desert living honed an Arab culture that is embodied in the Bedouin. Pride in this Arab Bedouin heritage and its legendary generosity and kinship, in addition to their role as guardians of the holy cities of Mecca and Medina, give modern Saudis the confidence to be leaders in the Islamic world.

Left and opposite: **Saudi Arabians are generally descended from the nomadic peoples of the Arabian Peninsula. There are few racial minorities in Saudi Arabia, and the population is essentially homogeneous.**

RACIAL MIXING

Some racial mixing did, however, occur along the fringes of the Arabian Peninsula. On the Red Sea coast, for example, some of the foreign pilgrims who came to Mecca from many parts of the world for the *hajj* stayed there and were absorbed into the indigenous population. Africans also migrated to this region. Thus, in Jeddah today, there are Saudis with Africanbackgrounds. Similarly, far to the east, migrants from Iran and India also settled down on the Persian Gulf coast and married the local people. Some Saudis in the Al-Hasa region today reflect this Persian and South Asian influence. Nonetheless, unlike the United States and some other countries, Saudi Arabia has never been a real melting pot of different cultures and peoples. While there are 5.36 million foreigners working in the Kingdom, they are not considered part of Saudi society.

The ethnic minority of Afro-Asians make up only 10 percent of Saudi Arabia's population.

A FEW PEOPLE IN A LARGE LAND

Saudi Arabia does not have a tradition of data-gathering. In a nomadic society, facts and figures simply did not have the importance they had in more urban cultures. In the early years of the Kingdom, data was hard to come by, but a 2002 census put the population at around 23.5 million people living in a land roughly two-thirds the size of the United States. Comparatively, the population in the United States in 2002 was an estimated 280 million.

The population in Saudi Arabia is also relatively young, with a median age of under 20 years. And with the population's high growth rate (somewhere between 2 and 4 percent each year), the number of children will continue to increase rapidly.

HONOR AND THE NEED TO SAVE FACE

Folklore from the Saudi past tells the story of a Bedouin sheikh who was known as the "Benefactor of the Wolves." Whenever he heard a wolf howling near his tent, he would order a servant to take a goat out into the desert, tether it there, and then return to the camp. The reason: the sheikh insisted on being a good host. "No guest," he is reported to have said, "shall call on me in the evening without dining." It would not be honorable, he felt, to let any guest—be it a camel or even a hungry wolf—leave his camp without being properly fed and given water to drink.

By greatly exaggerating the Saudi commitment to hospitality, this story points out the great importance of honor in Saudi culture. A desert warrior once remarked, "Bedouin can be roused to do anything for honor." The flip side of the coin of honor, however, is the need to save face, in other words, to preserve one's honor at all costs. Thus, even at the risk of bankrupting himself by his open-handed hospitality to all visitors, the sheikh felt he had to maintain his reputation as a generous host. Had he failed to do so, he would have been ashamed.

SOCIAL CLASS

The Prophet Muhammad proclaimed that all people are "equal children of Adam." He asserted that God does not pay attention to social rank or race but only to the sincerity of a person's beliefs and the works of charity performed during his or her lifetime. This belief in the fundamental equality of all is a cornerstone of Muslim social thought. Compared with many other societies in the world, there are surprisingly few overt signs of class distinction in Saudi Arabia today.

Nevertheless, social classes do exist. At the very top of the social pyramid is, as might be expected, the House of Saud itself, consisting of the many descendants of King Abdul Aziz. Next in line in the social hierarchy are the old merchant families. These families are often from Jeddah, and have amassed vast fortunes, which were derived from trade, that predate the oil boom. Although they have money, they have little political power.

Below them is a growing middle class of educated technocrats, small businessmen, and mid-ranking civil service officials. This group is becoming more important as national policies of "Saudization" (replacing foreign technicians with Saudi technicians) and diversification (developing sources of national income other than petroleum) begin to take hold. These officals are the Saudis with the most hands-on experience in the actual running of a modern state.

Manual labor is considered "ignoble," and as a result, Saudis usually refuse to do it. There is no Saudi blue-collar working class in the cities. Manual labor is provided by migrant workers. In rural areas, there are still the small farmers and in the deserts, the remaining nomads. These two interest groups may be at the lower rungs of the social ladder, but politically the royal family still needs their support to stay in power.

THE END OF AN ERA

Oil riches have meant the gradual passing of nomadic life. The glamor and romance of this roaming existence probably always seemed more attractive to foreigners and to urban Saudis than to the Bedouin themselves. Nomadic life originally developed out of sheer necessity— it was the only way people could survive in the desert. But it is such a hard way of life that few people would follow it voluntarily.

Perhaps only 5 percent of the Bedouin are still full-time nomads. The rest are now only semi-nomadic or have settled down permanently, a process actively encouraged by the government of Saudi Arabia through financial and other forms of help. Thanks to the government's policy of letting the oil wealth trickle down through the whole society, for the first time a new generation of Bedouin has other alternatives. Young nomads no longer have to follow in their fathers' footsteps. Some will choose to do so, but most will acquire the job skills of the modern world—driving trucks, serving in the National Guard, or working in the oil industry. As a result, their own descendants may learn about traditional Bedouin life only through tales told by their grandparents.

A SAUDI TALENT: ADJUSTING TO RAPID CHANGE

Since the oil boom of the 1970s, Saudi Arabia has undergone rapid social change. From a simple background that saw little change over many centuries, the country had found great riches that propelled it forward into modern times, practically overnight.

In a period of little more than 30 years, Saudi Arabia has built a nation that cares for its sick, educates its young, and provides a wide choice of industries in which its workforce can participate. Things we all take for granted, such as running water and electricity, now reach even the most remote corners of the Kingdom.

It is a fascinating sociological study to see how the average Saudi has embraced the modern age while maintaining his or her traditions. While the nation's great wealth has brought rapid and widespread changes, the Saudi family has remained intact. Young Saudis cruise the Internet and play video games, but also respect their parents and stay away from drugs. The elderly are cared for within the family unit, and most Saudi mothers stay home to raise their children and take care of the family's needs, rather than working outside the home.

Another anchor of stability in this storm of change has been Saudi Arabia's government. The House of Saud led the country even before the Kingdom of Saudi Arabia was established in 1932, thereby providing a continuity in government.

But perhaps the biggest influence that has facilitated a smooth transition into the modern age has been the country's deeply-rooted belief in Islam. While the government's conservative interpretation of Islam has upset some, it is also the main rudder that guides the country's policies and practices, as well as the social lives and conduct of Saudi Arabians throughout the country.

LIFESTYLE

MODERN SAUDIS take great pride in their Bedouin past and in the rapid economic development of their country that has occurred under the leadership of the royal family. They are strongly committed to the welfare of all members of their extended families. Their religion, Islam, is also very important to them. All these national characteristics have deep roots in Saudi culture.

THE FAMILY: FIRST, LAST, ALWAYS

Since Biblical times, the family has been the only safe haven in the hostile environment of the Arabian Peninsula. It was not until the creation of the Kingdom of Saudi Arabia in 1932 that there was any central authority to keep the peace and punish transgressors. Under these conditions, the family became supremely important. Individuals simply could not survive on their own.

Traditionally, "family" meant the extended family. Covering at least three generations, the extended family usually included the father and mother, their unmarried children, and their married sons who had wives and children of their own. Other relatives were often included, too. For example, a divorced woman could not live alone but would return to the house of her father or another male relative. By the same token, a widow would move in with her son or son-in-law. These extended families were usually very close and very large.

In Saudi Arabia today, this pattern is changing. Married children prefer to set up their own households if they can afford it. The classic three-generation extended family, all living under the same roof or in the same compound, is no longer the rule, especially in the cities. Nonetheless, the new, smaller nuclear family has managed to inherit at least four of the key characteristics of the traditional extended family.

Opposite: **A Saudi father enjoys a cup of coffee and the companionship of his son.**

63

A farmer and his son ride a donkey-drawn cart in Al-Hasa.

TRADITIONAL FAMILY STRUCTURE

The traditional family structure that has been adopted by modern Saudi Arabians consists of the following traits, among others:

First is the central importance of the patriarch of the family. Descent is patrilineal—children are identified only through their father as ibn or bin Khalid (son of Khalid) or bint Khalid (daughter of Khalid)—and the oldest male is the unquestioned head of the family, the patriarch. When family decisions are made, he is the one who finally decides what should be done after hearing the views of other members of the family. The mother has a great behind-the-scenes influence on her family, but she is not the formal decision-maker.

Traditional family structure

A second trait is that the survival and prosperity of the family itself is considered to be much more important than the wishes of any individual in it. Because of his seniority, the patriarch is thought to be the one most able to identify the best interests of the group. Other family members are expected to go along with his decisions no matter what their personal feelings may be. The individualism found in the United States and some other Western cultures has no place in the Saudi way of life, particularly if it is expressed by women.

A third holdover from the days of the extended family is that most social activities take place only within the family. Traditionally Saudi families did not often go to restaurants or to public events such as fairs and festivals. Non-official entertaining was done at home, which offered the advantage of privacy. Additionally, keeping up with all the achievements and setbacks of parents, brothers, sisters, children, and other relatives is almost a full time job. It requires a constant exchange of visits and does not leave much time for other social activities outside the family circle.

A last inheritance from the extended family is the most important—personal security. The family is still the real safety net of Saudi society. It is a matter of family pride and honor that members take good care of one another. A person may be old, sick, unemployed, divorced, widowed, or handicapped—whatever the problem, the family will provide emotional support and money.

In the past the tribal families of the Arabian Peninsula used to play much the same social role, though on a bigger scale, as the extended family does today. Tribal leaders gave their followers moral and financial support in life and avenged them when they were killed in battle by other tribes. Over the past 30 years, however, city life and the rapid economic development of the country have made these tribal ties less relevant to many Saudis.

All that is best in the Arabs has come to them from the desert: their deep religious instinct, which has found expression in Islam; their sense of fellowship, which binds them as members of one faith; their pride of race; their generosity and sense of hospitality; their dignity and the regard which they have for the dignity of others as fellow human beings; their humor, their courage and patience; the language which they speak, and their passionate love of poetry.

*—Wilfred Thesiger,
in* Arabian Sands

Royal lifestyles vary a great deal. Some princes have huge palaces and lead an extravagant jet-set life. Others live modestly and devote themselves to business or good works. But all members of the royal family understand very clearly that their own well-being is directly related to the well-being of the House of Saud. They therefore cultivate and nurture family relationships, consulting other family members and getting their approval before making any major decisions.

THE ROYAL FAMILY

The most dramatic example of the Saudi family as a source for mutual aid and protection is the royal family itself, with an estimated 6,000 family members. Like other families, the House of Saud takes pains to make sure that its foundations are firm to ensure the continuity of the family line.

Although King Fahd will remain the official ruler of Saudi Arabia until his death, his poor health and advanced age make it difficult for him to make daily decisions affecting the Kingdom. That task now falls to his half-brother Crown Prince Abdullah, who is the leader of Saudi Arabia in all but name. Power has been shared with a new generation, too. King Fahd's son Muhammad is the governor of the oil-rich Eastern Province. The late King Faisal's son Saud is the Foreign Minister of Saudi Arabia. And Prince Sultan's son Bandar (nephew of King Fahd) is Saudi Arabia's ambassador to the United States. These arrangements at the most senior levels ensure that political and military power will remain with the royal family.

Thanks to its preeminent political position, the House of Saud is in a much better position than lesser families to make sure that its financial position is secure. The staggering wealth of the royal family, however, must be spread around. Because King Abdul Aziz had so many children, the royal family is huge. As in other families, all these people have a claim, great or small, to a share of the House of Saud's riches. The more successful members must see to it that their poorer relatives are not penniless.

A GROWING MIDDLE CLASS

Not all Saudis are princes or nomads. Many Saudi men and women are now well-educated and form a prosperous middle class. Often educated in the United States, they know the culture of the West, but prefer to live and work in their own country. Their lifestyle is much closer to the Western model than to the traditional Arabian one. This new educated middle class may be the bridge between the petroleum-based Saudi Arabia of today and the more diversified, technically-proficient Saudi Arabia of the future.

The Saudi middle class live in houses with a limited number of rooms or in apartments. They usually own these houses or apartments, borrowing money to pay for them from Saudi banks, which give generous loans for just this purpose. The men hold government jobs or else go into private business. In most cases, women stay home, caring for the children. If they choose to work, they are encouraged to have vocations in science, languages, and the arts.

Even though this group of people may study or work in the West for considerable periods of time, they continue to respect the religious teachings and customs of their own country. They know that their travels abroad are for specific purposes only. Once their goals have been achieved, almost all of them will return to the Kingdom. This basic faithfulness to their own traditions and values makes it easier for them to readjust to the restrictions of Saudi culture when they return to their homeland.

Apartment living is a feature of modern Saudi life. As the cities get increasingly packed, high-rise buildings are constructed to accommodate the rapid urban population growth.

MEASURING TIME

Saudis have inherited from their nomadic past a very relaxed attitude toward most commitments based on time, such as business appointments, sports events, and social engagements.

In Saudi eyes, time is too often the master of Western culture. They themselves are much more comfortable with time as their servant. It is said that the "correct" time for a 10:00 A.M. meeting is not when the clock itself says 10:00 A.M., but when they themselves are able to get to the place where the meeting will be held.

This relaxed view about time is neatly summed up in the very common Arabic phrase, *In sha' Allah* (God willing), as in "I will meet you at the hotel at 10:00 A.M., *In sha' Allah*."

Time in Saudi Arabia is measured by the Islamic calendar. It takes as its starting point the Hijrah (July 16, in A.D. 622), when Muhammad moved from Mecca to Medina. From this beginning, time is subsequently reckoned according to the lunar calendar, which has 354 days. Years are designated A.H., which stands for *Anno Hegirae*, Latin for "the year of the Hijrah." By using comparative tables, A.H. dates can be translated into C.E. (Christian Era or Common Era) dates. For example, the year 1424 A.H. corresponds to 2003 C.E.

The weekend is also different in Saudi Arabia. Because Friday is a day of rest and prayer, the weekend falls on Thursday and Friday, not on Saturday and Sunday. This fact is frequently forgotten by businessmen and officials in other countries, who sometimes try, unsuccessfully, to telephone their Saudi counterparts during the Saudi weekend.

MIGRATION AND HOUSING

One consequence of the oil boom of the 1970s was a great migration of Saudis from the countryside to the cities. They were drawn there by the prospects of high-paying jobs, good schools and hospitals, and better opportunities for their children to learn business and administrative skills. This flow of people is still continuing today.

To help these migrants, the Saudi government provides subsidized housing, usually on the outskirts of the big cities, for low-income groups. Some poorer migrants are offered small building plots for them to build their own dwellings on. These are usually modest one- or two-story houses that are built in one corner of the property, which is enclosed by a high wall for privacy. The rest of the land is used for keeping sheep and goats and for parking motor vehicles. The Saudi government also offers interest-free loans to facilitate the construction of homes.

THE BEST HOSPITALS IN THE MIDDLE EAST

The royal family wants the country's oil riches to be shared with the general population. It thus provides free medical care, not only for Saudi citizens, but also for foreign Muslims who come to the Kingdom for the *hajj* (pilgrimage). When medical problems cannot be treated in the country, Saudi patients, plus a family member to keep them company, are sent at government expense to hospitals abroad.

The building of King Faisal Specialist Hospital and Research Center in Riyadh is a striking example of the improved system of Saudi healthcare. Its state-of-the-art facilities provide specialized treatment for patients who in the past would have had to be sent abroad. More than 1,200 staff are engaged in keeping medical standards high. The King Khalid Eye Specialist Hospital, also located in Riyadh, is one of the best and treats trachoma, an eye disease that can lead to blindness. Foreign doctors, nurses, and technicians serve in these hospitals. As more Saudis are trained in medical skills, they will eventually replace these foreign specialists.

Opened in 1975, the King Faisal Specialist Hospital and Research Center in Riyadh offers different specialized fields of treatment from heart disease to eye ailments and disorders of the nervous system. The hospital is also equipped with the latest diagnostic machines and one of the largest closed-circuit television systems in the world.

EDUCATION: AT HOME AND ABROAD

Traditionally education in Saudi Arabia involved memorizing and reciting large blocks of the Koran. Saudi educational policy today is still firmly grounded in the study of Islamic beliefs. It also tries to convince students that, since their country is providing free education for them (including generous scholarships to study abroad), they have a responsibility to support their country's traditions and policies.

Before the oil boom, Saudi Arabia had a high level of illiteracy. In the 1970s the Kingdom began to build an impressive array of new schools, ranging from kindergartens to universities, staffed by Saudis and foreigners alike. Except at the kindergarten level, boys and girls may not go to school together. Boys' schooling consists of kindergarten, primary, intermediate, secondary (high school), and tertiary (university) levels. After the first year

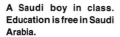

A Saudi boy in class. Education is free in Saudi Arabia.

of secondary school, boys may specialize in either scientific or literary studies. There are also vocational schools offering courses in technical, agricultural, and business subjects. Advanced studies take place at numerous colleges and universities, of which the new Diriyah campus of King Saud University is the largest and best known.

The Saudi government also pays for bright students to study abroad. Many Saudis who go to college overseas do so in the West, such as in the the United States, and to a lesser extent, the United Kingdom.

The first school for girls in Saudi Arabia was set up only in 1956. Before then, if they received any formal education at all, it was from private tutors in their own homes. Today, more than half of the nearly 200,000 students attending Saudi universities and colleges are women. Since they cannot attend classes with men, closed-circuit television is used so that they can listen to male lecturers. There are also some all-female campuses.

Young Saudis study at an elementary school for boys. Expanding formal education at all levels is a major concern for Saudi authorities.

Saudi women cloaked in the tradional black *abaaya* go shopping with their children.

THE SPECIAL WORLD OF SAUDI WOMEN

In a dramatic and unexpected move in 1990, a group of 70 veiled Saudi women defied the Kingdom's longstanding policy that women are not allowed to drive cars: they drove in a convoy of cars in Riyadh until the police stopped and detained them.

This remarkable demonstration for the right to drive was the first known public protest by Saudi women against the traditional role of women in the country.

Why does Saudi Arabia set what Westerners feel are such severe limitations on the freedom of women? The answer lies in one of the most important social values in Saudi Arabia—honor.

The honor of a man himself is inextricably bound up with the honor of the women of his family. In comparison with men, women are thought to be weaker and more subject to temptation. Moreover, the rules of behavior are so extremely rigid that a woman can jeopardize her sexual honor merely by talking to or sitting beside a man not related to her. Once violated, her honor can never be restored. Since the Koran teaches that men have authority over women, it is up to men to protect women. This is why women and men do not interact in public—to prevent any suggestion of inappropriate behavior that might shame a woman's family.

The result is that Saudi women are shielded by veil and social convention from all contact with men who are not their close relatives. They are not allowed to go to school with men, to work with men, to drive cars, or to appear in public dressed in a "provocative" manner, i.e. without being fully shrouded in a black *abaaya*. The socially preferred role for Saudi women is to be in the home. They are strongly encouraged to be wives, mothers, and homemakers. If women want to or must work, the most appropriate jobs for them are considered to be medical, social, or educational work, but only with women or girls as their patients, clients, or students.

These restrictions might not be tolerated by women in other societies, but few Saudi women protest these restrictions. With the solitary exception of the driving episode, there have been virtually no public protests by Saudi women. The reasons for this are not hard to find.

For one thing, Saudi women have been brought up to accept this way of life as entirely normal, and they earn the approval of their husbands and their families if they discharge their duties well. For another, they have virtually no alternative, except to leave the Kingdom and live and work in some other country. Also, by conforming to the demands of Saudi society, they are rewarded with a very high degree of personal, social, and financial security. And finally, consequences for non-conformity can be severe.

WEDDINGS: WOMEN'S WORLD

A young woman almost always accepts as her husband the man her parents have chosen. Her wedding is the most important day in her life and is celebrated elaborately. Wedding expenses are sometimes exorbitant, but the cost is shared by both families.

The private, religious part of the wedding is performed separately and before the more public ceremonial events. In Islam, the marriage ceremony itself involves an imam, or religious leader. He meets privately with the bride-to-be and asks her if she will accept the prospective husband. If she agrees, the imam later asks the groom, this time in the presence of four witnesses (who cannot be members of either family) if he will take the woman for his wife. If he says yes, this pronunciation, attested to by the witnesses, makes the marriage valid. The marriage contract is officially recorded by the imam.

At wedding celebrations, held in the evening at the bride's home or in a hotel, male and female guests do not mix. The men never see the bride, since it is quite unacceptable socially for an unveiled Saudi woman to be seen by men who are not her close relatives. Many Saudi brides now wear Western-style white wedding gowns. During the party, the bride and groom make a formal appearance among the female guests to receive their congratulations.

OLD AGE AND DEATH

The oldest man in a Saudi household is highly respected and has a great deal of power. As the senior male family member, he is the court of last appeal and decides what other family members should do to promote the interests of the family as a whole.

The oldest woman, for her part, does not have such a formal decision-making role, but can exert a powerful behind-the-scenes influence on such critically important family matters as choosing prospective brides or grooms for younger members of the family.

When the senior man is sick or incapacitated, all the other members of the family pool their knowledge and opinions to decide what should be done. The opinions of the senior male are also taken into account.

After a death, friends of the deceased may pay their condolences by calling on the bereaved family. When Saudis die, they must be buried within 24 hours—a sound policy in such a hot country. The custom is not to have elaborate funeral services even for very important people. In keeping with the nomadic tradition, the grave of King Abdul Aziz had no inscription and was marked only by two flat, upright stones at the head and foot of the burial mound. In 1975, when King Faisal was assassinated by a deranged nephew, he was buried simply and without fanfare in an unmarked grave in the desert. Winds and blowing sand soon erase any trace of a burial in Saudi Arabia.

An elderly Saudi.

RELIGION

SAUDI ARABIA is the birth-place of Islam, a religion that was first preached by Prophet Muhammad in the seventh century A.D. in Mecca and Medina. Islam has since grown tremendously and is now a major religion, with more than 1.3 billion believers all over the world. *Islam* in Arabic means "submission (to God)." Almost all Saudis are practicing Muslims, a name that signifies that they are believers, or followers, of Islam.

It would be very hard to exaggerate the importance of religion in Saudi Arabia today. The opening words of all official government documents are the opening words of the Koran: "In the name of Allah, the Compassionate, the Merciful." The very flag of the Kingdom bears the Muslim's declaration of faith: "There is no god but God; Muhammad is the Messenger of God."

One of the most common Saudi expressions is "*Alhamdulillah*" ("ahl-HAHM-doo-lee-lah"), meaning "Thanks be to God." No religion but Islam may be openly practiced in Saudi Arabia. And virtually everybody in Saudi Arabia, except for desert travelers, hears the melodious call to prayer five times daily.

Above: **Hajj pilgrims converge on Mecca.**

Opposite: **Pilgrims' tents at Arafat. Situated on a plain 10 miles (16 km) from Mecca, Arafat is the culmination of the hajj. This is where Muhammad preached his last sermon.**

A TOTAL WAY OF LIFE

It is often said that Islam is more than just a religion: it is a total way of life. Saudi culture adheres to a very strict interpretation of Islam. Islam permeates through all levels and aspects of society to the individuals themselves. Islam encourages a sense of brotherhood through a shared faith. It provides a set of regulations governing all aspects of family life and offers clear guidelines on personal behavior and legal matters. As a result, devout Muslims feel that they can find in Islam the answers to many of the pressing questions of everyday life.

Moreover, in Saudi Arabia there is no clear distinction, as there is in the United States and other countries, between church and state. The two are deeply intertwined; Saudi Arabia is an Islamic state governed by Islamic law and administered through Islamic social institutions.

THE *MUTAWA*

Religious laws and customs in Saudi Arabia are rigidly enforced at the street level and in the *souq* (SOOK) by the *mutawa* (MOO-tah-wah), or religious police.

Working for the politically influential Committee for the Propogation of Virtue and the Prevention of Vice, the *mutawa* are often older men with henna-dyed beards, who carry a camel whip as a token of office. Semi-educated younger men who reject Western culture are also in its ranks.

The *mutawa* are strict Muslims whose job is to make sure that stores close promptly at prayer times and that women appearing in public are properly dressed. A woman who is not wearing an ankle-length skirt or whose arms or legs are visible may get a whipping on her legs or arms from one of the *mutawa* to warn her against such "immodest" behavior in the future.

BASIC BELIEFS: GOD AND HUMANITY

Saudi Arabia is the cradle of Islam, a religion that is practiced by more than one billion people around the world. Compared with the polytheistic beliefs it replaced, the religion introduced by the Prophet Muhammad brought many social reforms and higher ethical standards to Arabian society.

ONE GOD Muslims believe that there is only one God, who created and sustains the world we live in. Muhammad himself was not divine but the last and greatest of a series of prophets. Jesus Christ, Abraham, and Moses are also revered as prophets in Islam.

PARADISE One of the prophet Muhammad's main teachings was that no matter how old you are or what your past sins have been, it is never too late to repent and ask God for forgiveness. Islam teaches that God judges everyone by their behavior during their lives. Those who live meritorious lives will get to enjoy the pleasures of heaven, which, with bountiful food and endless streams of pure water is just the opposite of the harsh daily life of the desert.

CHARITY Bound together by their common faith, Muslims should ideally be, according to Islam, a caring community. Islam stresses the importance of works of charity to ease human suffering, such as giving money to the poor. Muhammad himself had directed his followers to pay special attention to those who were in the greatest need in his own time: women, orphans, and slaves. Lending money at interest (usury) is forbidden.

Burning incense on Thursday night to welcome the holy day is a customary rather than a religious requirement.

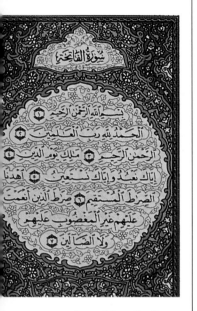

A *surah* from the Koran, the *al-Fatiha*, is recited by devout Muslims every day as part of their prayers.

WRITINGS OF ISLAM

Knowing something about the famous scriptures of Islam—the Koran and the Hadith—also helps us to understand this world religion.

THE KORAN The Koran is to Muslims a divinely-inspired, never-failing source of religious instruction and literary excellence. It is considered by Muslims to be the direct word of God, brought to Muhammad in small increments by the angel Gabriel over a period of 20 years. Muhammad received these messages from God through visions, and he would recite aloud to his followers what had been revealed to him.

Initially recorded by his disciples on whatever materials were conveniently at hand—pieces of paper, stones, palm leaves, bits of leather, camel bones—these recitations were assembled into the Koran, which consists of 114 chapters, called *surah* (SOO-rah), of different lengths. The chapters have short titles, such as *The Cow*, which refer to creatures or people mentioned in the *surah* itself.

Some of the *surah* are brief, poetic statements. Others are longer and more complex. After the death of Muhammad in A.D. 632, Muslims felt the need for an agreed text of the Koran.

Islamic scholars compiled from different sources, an authoritative text of this sacred book. They succeeded so well that the Koran is considered by virtually all Muslims, and by many non-Muslims as well, to be a religious and literary masterpiece.

THE HADITH With the text of the Koran decided once and for all, scholars could turn their attention to the sayings and traditions surrounding the Prophet Muhammad himself. These are collectively known as the Hadith (hah-DEETH), which means a report or a record of sayings or actions. They

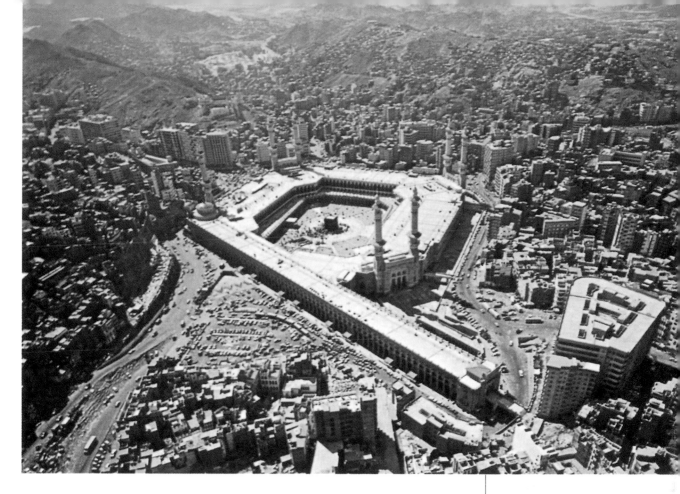

Aerial view of Mecca and the Grand Mosque with the Ka'bah, the focus of the annual pilgrimage.

offer detailed guidance to the faithful on almost all day-to-day activities of life, from how one washes oneself to how to forgive other people for wrongdoing by referring to the example of the Prophet and how he lived his life.

In the Hadith, tricky moral questions are asked and then cleverly answered. Here is a good example:

A man bought a piece of land and unexpectedly found a pot of gold buried there. Rather than secretly keeping the gold for himself, he immediately told the former owner about it. But the former owner refused the buyer's claim to the gold, saying that it had not been part of their bargain.

The solution, which was proposed by a third man called in to solve the problem, was truly creative: the son of the new owner should marry the daughter of the former owner. In that way, the young couple could then be given the gold as their wedding present!

THE FIVE PILLARS OF ISLAM

After Muhammad died in A.D 632, his followers began to define more formally what it meant to be a Muslim. They identified five key duties for members of the faith. Known as the Pillars of Islam, these are duties that every Muslim has to fulfill if he or she is able to.

The five pillars are: a declaration of faith, daily prayers, helping the poor, fasting, and a pilgrimage.

DECLARATION OF FAITH To become a Muslim, you must recite aloud a formal profession of faith, the *shahadah* (shah-HAH-dah): "There is no god but God; Muhammad is the Messenger of God." This is the first pillar. Once done, this act makes you a member of the believing community, and allows one to share fully in its religious creed and its daily way of life.

A café is closed for prayer. All offices and shops close up to half an hour at prayer times.

DAILY PRAYERS Praying five times a day is the second pillar. Believers are urged to pray together with others, but praying alone is also permitted if there is no alternative. The precise time for prayers changes daily, but they are always offered five times a day: before sunrise, in the early afternoon, in the late afternoon, after sunset, and before going to sleep.

Muslims can pray virtually anywhere: in the mosques, at home, in the desert, or at their places of work. In the afternoon, for example, it is common to see a row of praying men facing Mecca just outside the supermarkets of Saudi Arabia carrying out in unison the prescribed bows and prostrations of their prayers. Men can also pray in the aisle of an airplane, even when the plane is in flight. Women usually pray at home.

Attendance is encouraged at a weekly prayer service held at the mosques early on Friday afternoon. Here the imam, the leader of the service, takes a text from the Koran and elaborates on it in what can be a long, emotional sermon.

HELPING THE POOR The third pillar involves serving God by serving the needy. Known as *zakat* (ZAH-kaht), this act of social responsibility is fulfilled by donating a part of one's income to the poor. Normally it is 2.5 percent of an individual's net income annually. All Muslims are supposed to pay this tax, but since there are no penalties for failing to do so, it has become a voluntary offering.

FASTING The ninth month of the Muslim lunar calendar —which varies from year to year—is known as Ramadan. Fasting during the daylight hours of Ramadan constitutes the fourth pillar. (Since there were no clocks in the desert, early Muslims judged the exact time of sunrise as the moment when a white thread could be distinguished from a black one.) No eating, drinking, smoking, or sexual activities are permitted during the hours of the fast. Children, pregnant women, those who are ill, and those who are traveling are not obligated to fast.

THE PILGRIMAGE The fifth and last pillar of Islam is the *hajj*, the pilgrimage to Mecca all Muslims should make at least once if their health permits it, and if they can afford it. Each year, about 1.5 to 2 million Muslims from all over the world converge on Mecca by air, sea, and land to participate in one of the world's greatest pilgrimages. When Muslims have completed this pilgrimage, they are entitled to be known by the honorable title of *hajji* for men or *hajjah* for women.

Walkways connect the hills of Safa and Marwah that the pilgrims pass seven times as part of the *hajj* ritual.

RITES OF THE HAJJ

There are two kinds of pilgrimage to Mecca, Islam's most sacred city: the shorter *umrah* (OOM-rah) or visit, which can be done at any time of the year, and the *hajj* itself, which has a more elaborate ritual and takes place only once a year. The rites of the *hajj* require about 12 days to complete, but many pilgrims stay on longer to visit the other holy city, Medina.

As a first step of the *hajj*, before entering Mecca, the pilgrims put on special clothes signifying their holy state and their equality before God. For a man this outfit consists of unsewn white toweling and unsewn sandals; the only requirement for a woman is that she is not veiled. The pilgrims must also chant to God, showing acceptance of the rituals that lie ahead.

Entering the Grand Mosque of Mecca, the pilgrim walks seven times counter-clockwise around the Ka'bah, in which is set the Black Stone, a sacred relic believed by the faithful to date from the time of Abraham. Pilgrims kiss or gesture toward the stone, which is believed to be able to

Pilgrims collect pebbles to perform the ritual stoning of Satan, which takes the form of throwing stones at symbolic pillars.

absorb their sins. Other rites include drinking from the holy waters of the Well of Zamzam and a ritualized running (more like a brisk walk) between two low hills.

The culmination of the *hajj*, however, is the Standing on the Plain of Arafat, where pilgrims stand all afternoon reading from the Koran and repeating the prayer, "Here I am, O God, here I am!" The next day they gather pebbles to throw at three stone pillars, crying, *"Allahu Akbar"* ("ah-LAH-hoo akh-bar"), "God is most great!" Casting the stones symbolizes the casting out of evil. On the tenth day of the *hajj*, men shave their heads, and women cut a few stands of their hair. To commemorate Abraham's sacrifice of his son Ishmael, sheep or goats are sacrificed, and the meat is given to the poor.

At mosques around the world men and women are usually segregated, but during the *hajj*, both sexes may walk and pray together. Women, however, must be accompanied by a husband, a male relative, or by at least one other pious woman when they perform the *hajj*.

The Prophet's mosque in Medina is adorned with exquisite minarets and has ten major gates. It houses the Prophet's chamber, which contains the graves of the Prophet and his companions.

THE GREAT MOSQUES OF THE KINGDOM

From very modest beginnings, the great mosques of Saudi Arabia—the Quba Mosque near Medina, the Prophet's mosque in Medina, and the Grand Mosque of Mecca—have evolved into glorious destinations. They are at the same time places of prayer and centers for education.

Because Muslims are strongly encouraged to pray five times a day, mosques were traditionally built where most people congregated, in the middle of towns or near markets. Mosques vary in size and architectural design, but they have similar parts. The inner area of the mosque is designed for worship. The outer courtyard can also be used for prayers if the mosque itself is crowded.

Since Muslims are to pray facing the Ka'bah in Mecca, a *mihrab*, a recess in the mosque, shows the direction of Mecca. On Friday, sermons are given from a high pulpit inside the mosque. The melodious call to prayer is made from a tall minaret overlooking the mosque. In the past, the call was made

by a *muezzin* (moo-EZ-in) with a far-reaching voice. Today the *muezzin* uses loudspeakers.

The Quba Mosque, Islam's first mosque, was built by Muhammad in A.D. 622 before he entered Medina from Mecca. It has been upgraded many times, most recently by King Fahd in the early 1990s. In Medina, Muhammad built a second mosque, the Prophet's mosque, named after him. It, too, has been improved many times. In the late 1800s, for example, a lovely prayer hall and ornate colonnades were added.

Impressive as these two mosques are, however, the Grand Mosque of Mecca is the spiritual heart of Islam. It contains the Ka'bah, a cubic stone structure about 45 feet (14 m) high and 30 feet (9 m) wide, which is located in the center of the mosque. A huge black silk cloth, the Kiswah (KIS-wah), which is embroidered in gold with verses from the Koran, is draped over the Ka'bah and is replaced every year. Flanked by minarets 270 feet (82 m) high and often renewed and expanded, the Grand Mosque is a masterpiece of Islamic taste, craftsmanship, and design.

Located in the center of Mecca, the Grand Mosque has been rebuilt and enlarged several times and is today spacious enough to accommodate 600,000 worshipers.

LANGUAGE

SAUDIS SPEAK ARABIC, a Semitic language, related to Hebrew and Aramaic. One of half a dozen widely used international languages today, Arabic is spoken by over 120 million people spread over a large area that includes North Africa, most of the Arabian Peninsula, and parts of the Middle East.

Many Saudis believe that Arabic has a special importance because it is the language of the Koran. The verbal richness of the Koran has, for the Saudis, set a world standard for literary elegance. The wide range of subtle meanings that Arabic can express makes this language especially well-suited to poetry.

Arabic has two basic forms. The first is classical (written, or literary) Arabic, which is the same throughout the whole Arab world.

Above: **A bookshop sells Islamic literature. The expressive Arabic language is the vehicle of Islam and an important cultural legacy of the Arabic Peninsula.**

Opposite: **A sculpture in Jeddah is inspired by Arabic calligraphy.**

The second, spoken Arabic, varies considerably from one region to another. Translating Arabic words into other languages is quite difficult because the sound system of Arabic is very different from English and other European languages. Moreover, some of the sounds commonly used in Arabic are never used in Western languages. As a result, there are several possible ways in English to spell the same Arabic word, although some are seen as more authentic by Arabs. For example, "Moslem" and "Muslim" are both used, but "Muslim" is the preferred usage. "Muhammad" is also seen as "Mohammed." "Saud" might be more accurately represented in English as "Sa'ood." One author found no fewer than 16 different spellings for the Red Sea port of Jeddah.

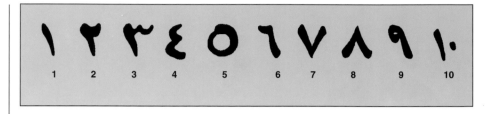

| 1 | 2 | 3 | 4 | 5 | 6 | 7 | 8 | 9 | 10 |

THE ARABIC ALPHABET, CALLIGRAPHY, AND NUMBERS

The Arabic alphabet was probably invented in the fourth century A.D. Thanks to the rapid rapid advance of the Arab empire after the death of Muhammad, the Arabic alphabet to spread quickly and is now the second most widely used alphabet in the world—the Latin alphabet is the most common.

The Arabic alphabet has 28 letters and is written and read from the right of the page to the left. The earliest copies of the Koran were written in a heavy, monumental script known as Kufi. About A.D. 1000, however, this style was replaced by Naskhi, a lighter script widely used in Saudi Arabia today. The form of this script is cursive, or a flowing style of writing that joins letters together.

In Saudi Arabia and other Islamic countries, calligraphy is a highly valued art because it is often used to copy the Koran, which Muslims believe contains the words of God. Calligraphers writing in Arabic use a reed pen with an angled point. This point lets them make bold downstrokes, narrow upstrokes, and all the variations between these extremes.

Kufi, Naskhi, and other regional scripts lend themselves extraordinarily well to a splendid calligraphy, whether written on paper or employed to adorn the walls of mosques and other buildings. In these latter cases, verses from the Koran are often carved into the walls or written on tiles, which are then glazed and set in the walls.

Many English words come from Arabic such as alchemy, alcohol, algebra, alkali, almanac, arsenal, assassin, azimuth, cipher, coffee, elixir, nadir, mosque, sugar, syrup, and zero. The numbers 0, 1, 2, 3, 4, 5, 6, 7, 8, 9, so familiar to us, are known as Arabic numerals. The Arabs initially learned them from the Indians and later passed them on to the West.

PERSONAL NAMES

Saudis may give a child as many as four names: his or her own name, the father's and grandfather's names, and a tribal or family name.

There is a wide range of personal names. Some typical names for Bedouin men are Khalaf, Sattam, Nayif, Mit'ib, and Rakan; some typical names for Bedouin women are Sitih, Wadha, Joza, Amsha, and Salma.

Among the settled, non-Bedouin Saudis, men's names include Salim, Salman, Nasir, Salih, and Saif; women's names include Miznih, Hissih, Haya, Mudi, and Zainab.

There are no family names as such among the nomads. Each person takes the name of the clan or tribe as his or her last name. Examples of such names are Al Harbi, Al Shammari, and Al Marri. Among the settled Saudis, however, family names are the rule, for example, Al Gublan, Al Jabir, and Al Bassam. ("Al" in this context means "dynasty" or "house of." Thus "Al Saud" means "House of Saud," i.e. the royal family.)

A Saudi man might be known as Muhammad bin Ahmad Al Sudairi (Muhammad, son of Ahmad of the Sudairi family), but in practice, he may be addressed simply as Muhammad or Mr. Al Sudairi. A woman takes her father's name and keeps it all her life, even after marriage. If she bears a son, *umm* is added to her name, followed by the name of her son, i.e. *umm* Ali (mother of Ali).

A group of Saudi boys pose for a picture. Saudi boys are commonly named after key figures in Islam.

BODY LANGUAGE

Within the circle of their extended family and with friends of their own sex, Saudis are warm, open people. Saudi men greet each other enthusiastically and may hold hands while walking together along a street—this is an expression of friendship. But in the presence of strangers, Saudis are usually much more restrained and are not given to any public displays of emotion.

When he shakes hands, a Saudi man prefers a short, limp handshake rather than a long, bone-crushing grip. After shaking hands with another Saudi, he may briefly bring his right hand to touch his heart as a show of his sincerity.

When a Saudi man meets another Arabic speaker, he will probably greet him with the traditional welcome, *"as-salam alaykum"* ("as-sahl-lahm ah-LAY-koom"), or "peace be upon you." The traditional response is *"wa-alaykum as-salam,"* meaning "and to you be peace."

Outside the extended family, men and women interact in separate social circles. When a husband and wife go to a party, the husband joins the men in one part of the house, while the woman joins the other women elsewhere. Outside their homes,

Saudis enjoy being hospitable and friendly to one another.

Saudi men and women never mingle with the opposite sex. Public displays of affection, even between husband and wife, are strictly forbidden.

THE MEDIA

The press, radio, and television are not free as in the United States, but are subject to government censorship. The government does not tolerate any criticism of Islam. "Pornography" such as advertisements showing women models wearing bras or panties is prohibited. There are several daily and weekly Arabic newspapers.

Aware of the basic role played by the information media in encouraging participation in development projects and in educating the citizens about their responsibilities and national duty, the government has made ample provisions for radio and television services. Programs now reach 90 percent of the country's population. Many of the programs are religious and literary in nature.

Most Saudis have satellite dishes that bring them uncensored news and entertainment programs from all parts of the world. The American news channel CNN is also widely viewed throughout the Kingdom. And more than 570,000 Saudis have access to information on the Internet.

LANGUAGES OTHER THAN ARABIC

Because of Saudi Arabia's relationship with Britain and the United States, English is widely spoken by educated Saudis, including military officers and merchants. Many of the foreign workers in the Kingdom do not speak Arabic, but do speak at least some English. As a result, since the 1970s English has become the *lingua franca* (common tongue) of business, aviation, medicine, transportation, and communications.

95

ARTS

MOSQUES AND POETRY are Saudi Arabia's two important contributions to the arts of the world. Other forms of Saudi art are restricted by a principle known as aniconism—the religious prohibition of representing any living creature by painting, sculpture, or other means. This prohibition stems from an Islamic belief that only God can create life. According to the conservative Saudi interpretation of this belief, an artist who produces an image of a living creature is trying to act like God. Saudi conservatives also fear that images might become idols and people might focus attention on the images rather than on God.

Some Muslim countries have not always rigorously followed the guiding principle of aniconism, but Saudi Arabia has always taken an uncompromising stand. Saudi purists also frown on large-scale public presentations of drama, fiction, songs, or instrumental music. As a result, the intellectual side of Saudi life is dominated by the spoken and written word and by Islam.

The nomadic life of the Saudis imposed its own strict logistical limitations on art since a Bedouin could own only what he could carry on his camel. Transporting paintings, drawings, or carvings from one grazing ground to another on camels would have been impractical.

Above: **Automobiles protrude from a huge concrete cube—an imaginative blend of art and technology in Jeddah.**

Opposite: **A modern fish sculpture in Jeddah's Corniche area. Sculpture is still not well received in most parts of Saudi Arabia especially by conservative Muslims, but a less strict approach to art and sculpture is being adopted in Jeddah.**

STORYTELLERS AND POETS OF THE DESERT

In pre-Islamic days, poetry was the highest form of art in the Arabian Peninsula, appreciated and loved by the nomads.

A rich oral tradition was part of the Bedouin culture. Tales of personal exploits and tribal conquests were passed down from generation to generation through stories, often in the form of poetry. These tales played an important role in preserving and shaping Bedouin history. Over time storytelling and poetry became a Bedouin heritage and legacy. Words were a nomad's favorite form of artistic expression. To be a poet was to hold a post of great honor. According to an 11th-century Muslim writer, whenever a poet emerged in an Arab tribe, other tribes would come and offer congratulations, for the poet was a defense to their honor, a protection for their good repute. He immortalized deeds of glory and published their eternal fame.

In the poverty of desert life, a man who could string words together in mystical chains telling tales of bygone days in a way that sang to the heart rather than the mind was indeed a man deserving of praise.

THE FUNCTIONAL ROLE OF THE ARTS

Given the prohibition on representational art, traditional Saudi artisans turned their attention instead to making everyday functional objects more beautiful. In this they succeeded, despite the limited natural resources at their disposal. Objects in daily use were carefully made and were decorated with geometric, floral, and calligraphic designs.

For example, handsome wooden incense burners perfumed tents and houses with the smoke of

frankincense; graceful brass water jugs were used to rinse the right hand before eating; roasted coffee beans and cardamon seeds were pounded in sturdy, elegant brass mortars; the resulting mixture was boiled in nicely decorated brass coffeepots; big wooden trays three feet in diameter were used to serve mutton and rice at banquets; chests, bowls, saddle frames, and other items made of wood were embellished with brass or silver nails; prayer beads, made from materials gathered from around the world, were traded in Mecca; house doors were ornately carved with geometric designs; narrow-necked pottery urns stored water or food; decorated leather goods, mats, and baskets, all well-suited to the tasks at hand, were also produced.

One unavoidable casualty of the modernization of Saudi Arabia in recent years has been traditional handicrafts. In many cases, handmade items have been replaced by cheaper mass-produced substitutes imported from abroad. Fortunately, however, many old pieces are still in daily use. Others can be found for sale at the *souq,* or traditional markets.

Gleaming brass coffee-pots and porcelain tea-pots with floral designs grace an Arabic shop.

Woven blankets, bags, and rugs are sold at a *souq*.

WEAVING AND EMBROIDERY

If poetry was a nomadic man's art, weaving and embroidery were part of the nomadic woman's world. One of the biggest tasks for Bedouin women was making the long tent. Known as "houses of hair," these tents were woven by hand from goat or camel hair, or from wool. On the outside the tents were black (goat hair in Saudi Arabia is jet-black), but the interior was decorated with colorful carpets. The carpets separated the tent into three sections: one for guests, where they were served coffee; another as a living space for family members and a storeroom for supplies; and the third as a cooking area.

Other woven items were also essential to nomadic life. Women made richly decorated riding litters, saddlebags, and tasseled blankets to use when traveling on camels. Woolen cloaks kept out the winter cold. Dresses were made from hand-loomed textiles. Carpets formed a floor for the tent, kept the sand at bay, and added touches of vivid color to the monochrome brown of desert life.

Embroidery was traditionally a skill learned by all young women. In the past almost all clothing in the Arabian Peninsula was embroidered by hand. Since the invention of the sewing machine, hand embroidery has given way to machine work.

The huge Kiswah (the ornate black cloth draped over the Ka'bah), which was formerly made in Egypt every year and presented to Saudi Arabia, is the largest, most important embroidered item now produced in the Kingdom. Each year, a new Kiswah is made by skilled embroiderers, using gold and silver metal thread on black velvet. The pattern consists of exquisite, flowing calligraphy of verses from the Koran, which is surrounded by interlaced patterns of leaves.

A carpet merchant shows one of his carpets to tourists. Carpets were first used as coverings for dirt floors and were a form of decorative art practiced by the nomadic people.

BEDOUIN JEWELRY

In a nomadic society without banks and with few material possessions, a woman's wealth was in her jewelry. A Bedouin woman received most of her jewelry when she married. Usually made from silver and studded with turquoise and red stones, it was melted down upon her death, to be recast later as new pieces in other traditional designs.

Bedouin jewelry comes in the form of ornate necklaces, bracelets, armlets, anklets, belts, nose and ear ornaments, and finger-rings and toe-rings. These are still made in Saudi Arabia by silversmiths, using techniques that have not changed much for hundreds of years. Metal is annealed (heated and then gradually cooled to make it soft and malleable), fused, cast, hammered, embossed, or engraved. Silver jewelry is often ornamented with filigree work—thin wire twisted into delicate patterns and soldered into place.

New jewelry is sold by the weight of its silver and stones, not by its workmanship. Imported machine-made items, being much cheaper to manufacture than handmade Bedouin jewelry, have in recent years been pricing traditional jewelry out of the market. Nevertheless, a good deal of used traditional jewelry is still available in the *souq* of Riyadh. Bargaining for it is a favorite pastime of many foreign residents.

Left: **L-shaped Bedouin dagger with its sheath in beautifully wrought silver.**

Below: **A Saudi merchant sells an assortment of daggers at a *souq*.**

ORNATE WEAPONS

Because of the dangers of desert life, men in Saudi Arabia were, until recent times, heavily armed. They carried spears, well-tempered swords, and camel-hide shields before rifles became widely available as a result of World War I.

When weapons were no longer needed for personal defense they were still carried for ceremonial and cultural reasons. This profusion of weapons offered unlimited opportunities for ornamentation and decoration. A man was not completely attired without at least a dagger at his waist. Silversmiths devoted themselves to embossing the hilts of swords and daggers. Sheaths for daggers received meticulous attention. Traditionally made of wood and encased in leather or cloth, they were finished with silver and semiprecious stones and carried in embroidered belts. Fine center-fire rifles from the West were engraved and decorated with gold. Traditional Arabian muzzle-loading rifles had graceful, curving wooden stocks often studded with brass decorations.

103

THE *ARDHA* (SWORD DANCE)

The *ardha* (ahr-DAH) is a traditional Arabian dance that is performed in public places on religious and festive occasions.

The dancers, all men, are dressed in flowing white robes and armed with long swords (*below*). They stamp heavily and flash their swords, hopping from one foot to another in time to the African-like beats and rhythms of the accompanying drums and tambourines.

As part of the performance, young girls under 12 years old ululate, or utter high-pitched, wordless wailing. Wearing long bright dresses, they sway in time to the music and flick their long hair, which is heavily ornamented with beads, from side to side.

The audience may clap along or even join in the dance. When male members of the royal family are present they sometimes join the *ardha* dancers. When they do, they not only enjoy themselves, but they pay public tribute to the memory of how their ancestor, King Abdul Aziz, won Saudi Arabia—by the sword.

The dance has its origins in the Najd. Today the government of Saudi Arabia has set up several cultural institutions that promote and preserve Saudi Arabia's rich cultural heritage. The *ardha* dance is also performed in theaters.

ARCHITECTURE OF THE PAST

The most dramatic ancient ruins in Saudi Arabia are the well-preserved tombs and buildings carved into solid rock at Madain Salih in the northwest of the country. These are more than 2,000 years old and were built by the Nabateans, an ancient nomadic people who once prospered as middlemen in the Arabian Peninsula's spice trade.

During the early years of Islam, architecture was simple and functional. Mosques began as minimal structures and only later evolved into their present glory. In the past only the rich had houses made of stone. The less fortunate had to be content with homes made of sun-dried mud bricks, which were cheap to make, easy to repair, and kept dwellings cool in the summer and warm in the winter. Roof structures were usually made of tamarisk. Thick-walled forts and palaces were also made of these coarse, sunbaked mud bricks, which were durable and strong. The historic fortified palace in Riyadh, Qasr al-Masmak, which Abdul Aziz captured in 1902, is a good example.

Traditional mud brick houses can still be found in Najran. The rooftops serve as terraces where families can relax.

The many-spired Heritage Museum in Riyadh, with its large collection of antiquities, is an exquisite complex built in the traditional style. It has intricately built facades adorned with carved wooden windows and balconies.

MODERN INTERPRETATION OF TRADITIONAL ARCHITECTURE

The old houses of Jeddah were architecturally quite remarkable. These houses were often two to four stories high and had windows and balconies with elaborately carved wooden screens that provided both privacy and ventilation. Women could sit in proper seclusion behind these screens and still be able to see what was going on in the narrow streets below. In the wetter parts of the Asir region, pieces of slate were set at an angle into whitewashed walls to protect the walls from damage caused by hail and heavy rain.

With the rapid development caused by the oil boom, a large number of modern buildings have been built. What is interesting about these buildings is that many have combined traditional Saudi styles with modern materials. This successful integration is best exemplified by many of the buildings in Riyadh. Among the most striking are the Royal Pavilion at King Khalid International Airport, the United Nations Building, and the spectacular King Fahd International Stadium, which is one of the largest stadiums in the world.

Many modern apartment buildings have adopted the carved wooden screens of the traditional Jeddah houses. Besides being aesthetically appealing, the screens serve to keep the house cooler during the day by permitting cool breezes to pass through while shading the interior from intense sunlight.

King Khalid International Airport is an eclectic blend of the traditional and modern.

LEISURE

FOR SAUDIS most entertainment takes place in the home and involves the family and relatives. There is not much public entertainment in Saudi Arabia. There are no pubs or bars because alcohol is banned under Islam. Saudi men and women are not supposed to mix socially, which rules out movies, restaurants, plays, art exhibitions, and many other cultural activities that adults of both sexes might conceivably attend.

Spending time with one's own family, keeping in close contact with other members of the extended family, celebrating birthdays, arranging marriages, catching up on the latest family gossip, and watching television and videos—these are favorite Saudi pastimes. Some Saudis participate in sports, and those who can afford it take vacation trips to countries with a cooler climate.

Left: **Like their desert ancestors, modern Saudis attach a great deal of importance to the family. Most of their leisure time is spent with other family members.**

Opposite: **Young camel riders receive their prizes at a camel race. An annual event, camel races attract many spectators, and even members of the royal family.**

109

FESTIVALS

SAUDI ARABIA has two nationwide seasons of merrymaking each year. Both of these holidays, which are known as the Eids (eeds), are important religious and family celebrations.

One other day that is commemorated officially, the Saudi National Day, marks the unification of the Kingdom of Saudi Arabia in 1932.

The Saudis do not celebrate the birthday of the Prophet Muhammad, nor do they hold regional festivals. In their private lives, however, they do celebrate family events such as the birth of a child or a wedding.

THE TWO EIDS

EID AL-FITR The first of the two annual national holidays, Eid al-Fitr (eed ahl-FITTER), the Feast of the Breaking of the Fast, is also known as Eid al-Sagghir (eed ahl-sahg-HEER), the Little or Lesser Festival. It celebrates the end of the demanding month-long Ramadan fast. Going without food or drink during the long, hot hours of the desert day from sunrise to sunset is never an easy matter. As a result, the end of the Ramadan fast is a time of happiness and rejoicing.

The exact date of this Eid is never known precisely in advance because it depends on the proper sighting of the moon the night before the festival begins. Sometimes the Eid is announced after midnight, after the children have gone to bed. This makes the celebration a time of suspense for them.

Below: **Mosques are crowded on religious holidays like the Eids. Besides visiting friends and relatives, Muslim families visit mosques to pray and give thanks.**

Opposite: **Children are dressed in their best on Eid al-Fitr, which celebrates the end of the fasting month.**

FOOD

SAUDI ARABIANS like to eat well. Whether they are sitting on chairs and eating Western-style food with knife and fork, or squatting on the floor eating a traditional feast of mutton and rice with their fingers, the big serving table is well covered with delicious foods.

Arabs have a strong tradition of hospitality. At a meal, offering several different kinds of food in large quantities is considered good manners. So is setting the table nicely, if possible with elegant silver utensils, and decorating it with bowls of fresh fruit. Saudis love to eat fresh fruit. Grapes, oranges, figs, dates, melons, cherries, and apricots are a common sight on a Saudi table. This lavish hospitality shows the generosity of the host and hostess and their concern for the welfare of their family or guests. Having lots of food in large portions is also a way Saudis show that they honor their guests.

One type of food and a type of beverage are strictly forbidden to Saudis: pork, because it comes from pigs, which are considered unclean by Muslims; and alcohol, which Muslims are not supposed to drink. The prohibition for eating pork or drinking alcohol is stated in the Koran.

Since Muslims are not permitted to consume alcohol, fruit and vegetable juices are popular alternatives. All sorts of fruit and vegetables are used to make juices that are healthy as well as thirst-quenching. Fruit and vegetable concentrates are also readily available in cans and bottles.

Below: **A typical Saudi dish of rice with ground lamb and nuts.**

Opposite: **A public fruit market.**

A brass coffeepot, coffee seeds, and small cups for serving coffee stand on a table. Coffee drinking is a social institution in Saudi Arabia, and preparing it is an art.

THE COFFEE AND TEA RITUAL

In Saudi Arabia coffee plays an important role as a social lubricant. To this extent, it takes the place that alcohol occupies in other countries. Coffee is served to guests as soon as they arrive. Men meet at the local coffee shop to discuss the day's events. Feasts end immediately after coffee has been served. Because it stimulates people physically and socially, coffee has been used for a long time in the Arabian Peninsula. In fact, some believe that coffee originated here, near Mocha in Yemen, where fine coffee is still grown.

There is a special way to prepare coffee in Saudi Arabia. A small handful of green coffee beans are roasted over a fire. With a pestle, the beans are then pounded in a brass mortar and flavored with cardamon seeds. Water is then added. The coffee is brought to a boil three times, each time in a different brass pot, and is finally poured out by a servant in a long arching stream into tiny cups. The cups are filled only halfway. The custom is never to accept more than three cups; holding out the cup to the server and tilting

A fast-food outlet in Jeddah serves pizza.

it from side to side is the sign that you have had enough, and that the server should take away your empty cup.

Small cups of heavily sweetened tea are often offered to visitors as well. There is no special technique involved in brewing tea, but the same basic rule applies: drinking more than three cups is considered bad manners.

SHAWARMA AND OTHER FAST FOODS

Shawarma (shah-WAHR-mah) is a delicious Middle Eastern fast food sold in the *souq* and elsewhere in cities and towns in Saudi Arabia. It consists of slivers of roasted lamb carved from a spit, which is slowly rotated in front of a hot grill so that the meat is equally browned all over. Making a pocket of flat Arabic bread, the seller adds parsley, lemon juice, tomatoes, and spices and presents the *shawarma* to you with a smile.

In addition to this traditional snack, Western fast food is also available. It is popular in Saudi Arabia for the same reasons it is elsewhere—it is quick, filling, and cheap.

ETIQUETTE AND TABLE MANNERS

Genuine friendships based on mutual trust and appreciation are extremely important in Saudi Arabia. They open bureaucratic doors that would otherwise stay closed.

When a Saudi wants to entertain a foreign businessman, he will often invite him for lunch at home. Members of the extended family, on the other hand, are frequently entertained at home in the evening.

A male guest will be introduced to a Saudi's sons and to his young daughters, but he will neither see nor meet his wife or any older daughters. It is considered improper for a man to inquire about another man's wife. Thus the innocent American question, "How's your wife?" would not be well received in the Kingdom. Instead guests may appropriately ask how the sons or young daughters are.

Saudis do not like to call strangers by their first name until they know each other very well and have become friends. A Saudi man who is old and venerable or a young man from a good family may be accorded the honorary title of sheikh. If so, he will be addressed by it. An example is Sheikh Yamani. Otherwise, a man will be addressed as *Sayed* (sah-EED), or Mr.; a married woman is referred to as *Sayedah* (sah-eed-DAH), or Mrs.

At meals there are three main taboos. Since the left hand is considered unclean, only the right hand may be used for eating or for passing food or drink.

The soles of the feet are also considered unclean; it is offensive to point them at another person. At a traditional meal where there are no chairs and guests must sit on the floor, they should squat or sit so the bottoms of their feet do not face another person.

And, finally, it is impolite to stare at other people while they are eating. Looking down at your own plate instead is considered good manners.

Eating a greasy dish like mutton and rice with fingers takes practice and, for one not used to it, is difficult to do gracefully. It is extremely important to use only the fingers of the right hand. The best, and in fact the only, technique for eating politely with fingers is to make a small, compact ball of rice and small pieces of meat, using the fingers and thumb of the right hand. This little ball of rice and meat is then deftly popped into the mouth with the thumb.

ARABIAN BREAD

Saudis eat a delicious mottled bread covered with bran. The mottled effect is achieved by grilling the bread.

1 teaspoon sugar
1 cup warm water
$1\frac{1}{2}$ ounces (43 g) active dry yeast
1 cup (230 g) wholemeal wheat flour
$\frac{3}{8}$ cup (85 g) strong white wheat flour
$\frac{1}{2}$ cup (114 g) light rye flour
1 tablespoon salt
$\frac{1}{2}$ teaspoon cumin powder
1 tablespoon oil
bran

Dissolve the sugar in half a cup of warm water. Stir in the yeast gradually so that lumps do not form. Leave the solution in a warm place.

Warm a large mixing bowl by placing it in hot water, then dry it. Pour all of the three kinds of flour into it. Add the salt and cumin powder, and mix well. Pour in the dissolved yeast and the remaining water. Knead the dough for 10 to 15 minutes until the dough is smooth and elastic (it should not stick to your hands).

Remove the dough from the mixing bowl and pour oil into the bowl. Roll the lump of dough in the oil so that it has a light coating of oil. Put the dough in a plastic bag and set it aside for about two hours or until the dough doubles in size.

Heat a nonstick grill pan on high heat. Spread some bran on a large tray and set it aside. Knead the dough well, and divide it into seven pieces. Knead each piece in your hand, and flatten it into a disc. Place each disc in the tray of bran to coat only one side of the disc. Cook one disc at a time in the hot grill pan for about 4 minutes, turning over to the other side when done. The bread should look puffy and golden brown.

HUMMUS BI TAHINA

This is served as a *mezzeh* (MEH-zeh), a starter or appetizer in Saudi Arabia and other Middle Eastern countries. *Hummus bi tahina* is made from chickpeas and tahini.

18-ounce (225-g) can of chickpeas
2 tablespoons tahini or sesame seed paste (stir well)
1 clove garlic
juice of 1 lemon
3 tablespoons olive oil
1 teaspoon salt to taste

Mix all the ingredients together in a mixing bowl. (If you are unable to buy tahini, you can make it. Get ¼ cup of sesame seeds. Fry the seeds lightly or until fragrant, and pound it to a paste.) Blend all the ingredients in a food processor until smooth. Add a little water or more lemon (to taste) if the mixture is too thick. Pour blended mixture onto a plate or in a shallow bowl. Drizzle with a little olive oil, and garnish with some chopped parsley. There are many ways to enjoy hummus bi tahina. You can serve it as as a dip with cut vegetables, such as celery and cucumber sticks. It is also delicious with pita bread. Refrigerate leftovers.

BAKLAVA

Baklava is a sweet dessert made from thin layers of pastry stuffed with chopped nuts and drizzled with sweet syrup. It may be served hot or cold.

2 cups sugar
1½ cups water
1½ tablespoon lemon juice
5 whole cloves
2 cups chopped nuts (walnuts, cashew nuts, or pistachios)
2 teaspoons ground cinnamon
1 pound (450 g) unsalted butter, melted
1 pound (500 g) filo pastry (This can be purchased frozen from the supermarket. Follow the directions on the packet. Cover the filo sheets with a moist towel to prevent drying.)

Combine the sugar, water, lemon juice, and cloves in a saucepan. Bring to a boil over a medium heat for about 10 to 15 minutes, stirring constantly until it thickens to a syrup. Remove from fire and set aside to cool. Preheat oven to 350°F (177°C). Mix the nuts and the ground cinnamon in a mixing bowl. Lightly grease a 13- by 9-inch (33- by 23-cm) baking tray with some melted butter. Line the tray with a layer of the filo pastry. Grease the filo pastry with melted butter, and sprinkle some nuts on top. Repeat the process of forming layers until all the pastry sheets are used. Brush the top layer with butter. Cut the pastry into diamond-shaped pieces with a sharp knife. Bake in the oven for at least one hour until golden brown, then remove from the oven. Pour the syrup on top, and let the syrup soak into the pastry for a few hours before serving.

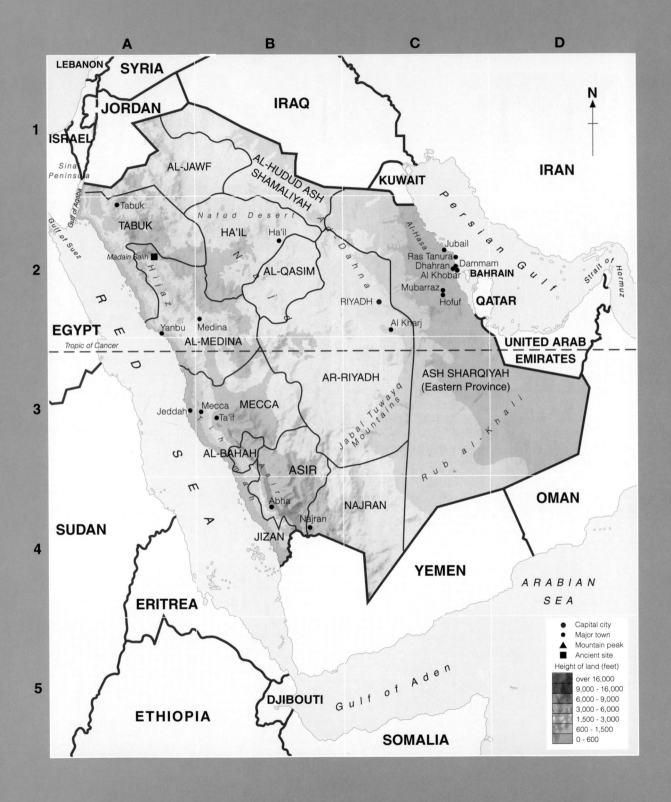

LEBANON SYRIA

A **B** **C** **D**

JORDAN

IRAQ

ISRAEL

1

Sina Peninsula

Gulf of Aqaba

KUWAIT

Persian Gulf

IRAN

N

AL-JAWF

AL-HUDUD ASH
SHAMALIYAH

• Tabuk

Nafud Desert

TABUK

HA'IL

Ha'il •

Al-Hasa

Jubail
Ras Tanura •
Dhahran • • Dammam
Al Khobar

Madain Salih ■

Hijaz

Gulf of Suez

AL-QASIM

Ad Dahna

2

RED

EGYPT

Yanbu • Medina •

AL-MEDINA

RIYADH •

Mubarraz • •
Hofuf •

BAHRAIN

QATAR

Al Kharj •

Tropic of Cancer

UNITED ARAB

EMIRATES

SEA

AR-RIYADH

ASH SHARQIYAH
(Eastern Province)

3

Jeddah • Mecca •
• Ta'if

MECCA

*Jabal Tuwayq
Mountains*

Rub al-Khali

OMAN

AL-BAHAH

Asir

ASIR

SUDAN

Abha •

NAJRAN

Najran •

JIZAN

4

YEMEN

*ARABIAN
SEA*

ERITREA

5

ETHIOPIA

DJIBOUTI

Gulf of Aden

SOMALIA

• Capital city
• Major town
▲ Mountain peak
■ Ancient site
Height of land (feet)
over 16,000
9,000 - 16,000
6,000 - 9,000
3,000 - 6,000
1,500 - 3,000
600 - 1,500
0 - 600

Strait of Hormuz

MAP OF SAUDI ARABIA

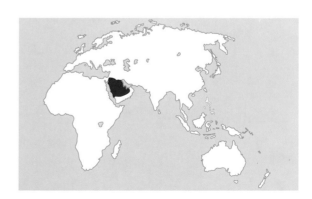

ECONOMIC SAUDI ARABIA

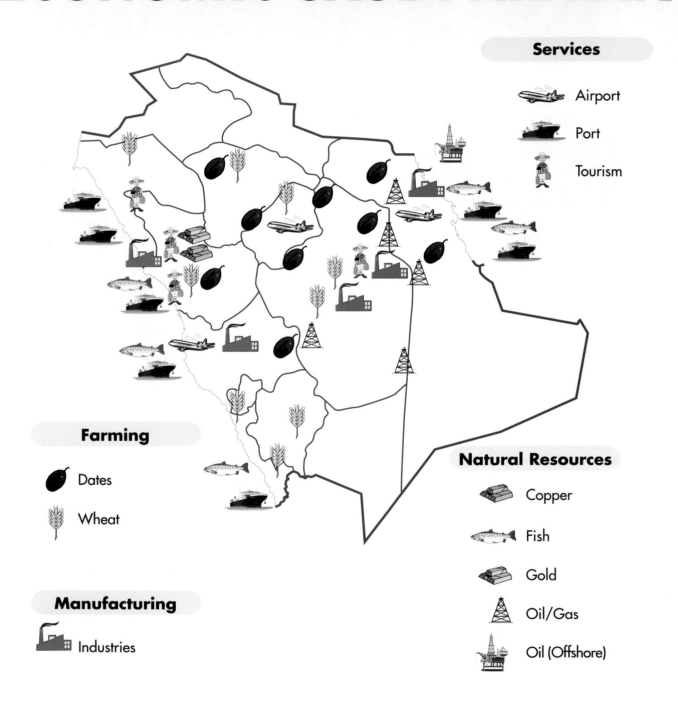

Services

✈ Airport

🚢 Port

🧑 Tourism

Farming

🫒 Dates

🌾 Wheat

Manufacturing

🏭 Industries

Natural Resources

Copper

Fish

Gold

Oil/Gas

Oil (Offshore)

ABOUT THE ECONOMY

OVERVIEW
Saudi Arabia has an oil-based economy. It has the largest petroleum reserves in the world and is the largest exporter of petroleum. The government is encouraging private-sector growth to lessen the country's reliance on the petroleum industry.

GROSS DOMESTIC PRODUCT
US$232 billion (2000 est.)

LAND AREA
756,982 square miles (1,960,582 square km)

LAND USE
Arable land 2 percent, others 98 percent

NATURAL RESOURCES
Petroleum, natural gas, iron ore, gold, copper

AGRICULTURAL PRODUCTS
Wheat, barley, tomatoes, fruit, sheep, chicken, and dairy produce

CURRENCY
1 Saudi Arabia Riyal (SAR) = 100 halalah
5 halalah = 20 qurush
USD$1 = SAR 3.75 (March 2003)
Notes: 1, 5, 10, 50, 100, 500 Riyal
Coins: 1, 2, 5, 10 qurush; 5, 10, 25, 50 halalah

LABOR FORCE
7 million

LABOR FORCE BY OCCUPATION
Agriculture 12 percent, industry 25 percent, services 63 percent (1999)

MAJOR EXPORTS
Petroleum and petroleum products, plastics, metal goods, construction materials, and electrical appliances

MAJOR IMPORTS
Food, beverages, tobacco, manufactured goods, machinery, and automobiles

MAJOR TRADE PARTNERS
The United States, Japan, Germany, South Korea, the United Kingdom, Singapore (2000)

PORTS AND HARBORS
Dammam, Dhiba, Jeddah, Jizan, Jubail, Rabigh, and Yanbu

AIRPORTS
209 total; 71 with paved runways (2001)

INTERNATIONAL PARTICIPATION
Gulf Cooperation Council (GCC); International Monetary Fund (IMF); Organization of the Petroleum Exporting Countries (OPEC); United Nations (UN); United Nations Educational, Scientific, and Cultural Organization (UNESCO); World Intellectual Property Organization (WIPO); World Health Organization (WHO)

TIME LINE

IN SAUDI ARABIA	IN THE WORLD
	753 B.C. Rome is founded.
	116–17 B.C. Roman empire reaches its greatest extent, under Emperor Trajan (98–17).
100 B.C. Nabateans begin building Madain Salih.	
A.D. 106 Romans capture the town of Petra to control trade routes. Nabatean civilization begins to decline.	
570 Prophet Muhammad is born in Mecca.	**A.D. 600** Height of Mayan civilization
610 Year of the *Hijrah* and the birth of the Islamic calendar	**1000** Chinese perfect gunpowder and begin to use it in warfare.
1400s Mamluks control the Hijaz region, including the holy cities of Mecca and Medina.	
1517 Ottoman Turks gain control of the Hijaz.	**1530** Beginning of trans-Atlantic slave trade organized by the Portuguese in Africa.
	1558–1603 Reign of Elizabeth I of England
	1620 Pilgrim Fathers sail the *Mayflower* to America.
1750 Muhammad bin Abdul Wahab and Muhammad bin Saud join forces to purify Islam.	**1776** U.S. Declaration of Independence
	1789-99 French Revolution
1818 Ottoman Turks capture the Saud ancestral home.	

IN SAUDI ARABIA	IN THE WORLD
	1861 U.S. Civil War begins.
	1869 Suez Canal is opened.
1891 The powerful Rashid dynasty seizes Riyadh.	
1902 Abdul Aziz Ibn Saud recaptures Riyadh in a fierce battle.	**1914** World War I begins.
1932 Unification of Arab tribes to form the Kingdom of Saudi Arabia	
1938 Discovery of oil at Dammam	**1939** World War II begins.
1945 Saudi Arabia signs the United Nations Charter.	**1945** United States drops atomic bombs on Hiroshima and Nagasaki.
1953 King Abdul Aziz dies; his eldest son, Saud, becomes king.	**1949** North Atlantic Treaty Organization (NATO) is formed.
1960 Organization of Petroleum-Exporting Countries (OPEC) is formed.	**1957** Russians launch Sputnik.
1964 King Faisal becomes king when his brother Saud abdicates.	**1966–69** Chinese Cultural Revolution
1981 Saudi Arabia becomes a founding member of the Gulf Cooperation Council.	**1986** Nuclear power disaster at Chernobyl in Ukraine
1990 Gulf War—Iraq invades Kuwait.	**1991** Break-up of the Soviet Union
1996 Khobar Towers housing complex is destroyed by suicide bombers.	**1997** Hong Kong is returned to China.
	2001 World population surpasses 6 billion.